P9-DBZ-948

HOW TO

HAVE A GREEN THUMB

WITHOUT

AN ACHING BACK

A New Method of Mulch Gardening

RUTH STOUT

Illustrated by Leta MacLeod Brunckhorst

A Fireside Book
Published by Simon & Schuster, Inc.
New York

Copyright © 1955, 1968, 1973 by Ruth Stout
All rights reserved
including the right of reproduction
in whole or in part in any form
First Fireside Edition, 1987
Published by Simon & Schuster, Inc.
Simon & Schuster Building
Rockefeller Center
1230 Avenue of the Americas
New York, New York 10020
Published by arrangement with the Exposition Press Inc.
Previously published by Simon & Schuster, Inc., under the
Cornerstone Library imprint.
FIRESIDE and colophon are registered trademarks
of Simon & Schuster, Inc.
Manufactured in the United States of America.
10 9 8 7 6 5 4 3 2 1 Pbk.
Library of Congress Cataloging in Publication Data
Stout, Ruth.
    How to have a green thumb without an aching
back.

    "A Fireside book."
    1. Gardening. 2. Mulching.   I. Title.
II. Title: Mulch gardening.
SB453.S689   1987   635   87-4324
ISBN 0-671-64061-5 Pbk.

CONTENTS

A Lilac Bush and an Apple Tree

When my husband and I are alone in the evenings I lie on the couch over by the fireplace and read. Fred is stretched out in his green leather chair on the opposite side of the big living room. If I mutter to myself he doesn't even look up from his book. He knows what is wrong: I'm exasperated at some statement about gardening I'm reading which contradicts my own experience.

Through the years my mutterings kept changing as I kept gathering first-hand knowledge. They began with: "Oh, I did that all wrong." Then: "How interesting!"—"How surprising!"— "I wonder?"—"That sounds cockeyed."—"Oh, for the love of Mike!"—"Ridiculous!"—"Is he crazy? Why doesn't he wake up?" Naturally, I read many things I agreed with, but when I agreed I didn't growl.

I have finally come to the conclusion that a lot of people who write on this inexhaustible subject are armchair gardeners, and after twenty-five years of experience in growing things my opinion is that armchair gardeners can say some very peculiar things.

My ambition is to write this book without a single statement which can be muttered at. I will try to accomplish this by relating my own experiences, letting the reader do the conclusion-drawing.

This does not mean, however, that my mind isn't crowded with opinions and convictions. It is. For instance, eleven years ago I put into practice a revolutionary method of gardening, and if I were put in charge of the world I would make it compulsory for every gardener to give it a three-year trial. After three years I don't believe anyone would go back to the old, cumbersome procedure. If someone did, if someone deliberately chose to work ten times as long and as hard as he needed, chose to spend more money and have more headaches than necessary with less satisfactory results, I wouldn't interfere. I doubt if there would be enough of them in the whole world to fill a medium-sized mental institution.

This method is described in detail in Chapters Six and Seven. In Chapter Eight you will find an easy and effective way to grow strawberries. I would not try to force this idea on anyone for, in my experience, it sells itself automatically to anyone who sees it or has it explained to him. So if I were running the world I wouldn't make that a law, but simply broadcast it.

The first five chapters are a story of the struggles I went through and the things I learned during the early years of gardening. I am hoping that someone may benefit by this account of my mistakes and triumphs, my heartaches and enchantments.

If "heartache" sounds exaggerated then surely you have never gone to your garden one rare morning in June to find that the frost, without any perceptible motive, any hope of personal gain, has quietly killed your strawberry blossoms, tomatoes, lima and green beans, corn, squash, cucumbers. A brilliant sun is now smiling at this disaster with an insensitive cheerfulness as out of place as a funny story would be if someone you loved had just died.

And if "enchantment" sounds a little farfetched you have not yet opened your eyes and heart to the unassuming miracle of the performance of a tiny seed as insignificant-looking as a fleck of dust. If you put a tomato seed, for instance, into the earth, and barely cover it, it will send a tender green shoot up through the soil. You can help it to do this with less strain if you cover it for a few days with a board, strip of cardboard, gunny-sack, or anything to keep it moist and prevent the light from reaching it.

But you must watch it. As soon as you see the shoot breaking through the ground the cover must come off. Then this little, live thing keeps getting bigger and greener and more and more surprising. It covers itself with green leaves and later with yellow blossoms. Did you ever stop to wonder how it decided always to have them yellow?

Soon the blossoms fall off and, amazingly enough, tiny green balls appear. These keep getting bigger and fatter.

Now, the next step would be hard to believe if you hadn't been taking it for granted all your life. These balls, having reached their full size, look about them, see that green is the predominant color in their environment and decide to break the monotony. They begin to experiment, try a touch of white, then greenish-yellow, then pink, and finally a bright, gay red. This furnishes an attractive contrast to their leaves, which keep their original green color.

At last these pretty balls have reached maturity; they are satisfied with what they have achieved and relax. They wait for the kind person who gave that tiny seed an opportunity to fulfill its greatest possibilities to come and eat them.

We call these little balls "tomatoes." To me it is almost awesome to look at a tiny tomato seed and then at a large healthy plant, heavy with green, pink and red tomatoes, and think of the completely reliable mystery involved.

A gardener has so many enemies, from a quiet little aphis to a big blustering hurricane, there is so much ignorance and misinformation to lead him astray, that it is comforting to have one thing he can count on. Any one seed may be too old to sprout or inferior in some way, but it will never try to be something it isn't fitted to be. A man may study to be a surgeon when he should have been a shoemaker, a talented painter may spend his life trying to convince himself and his fellows that he is a lawyer, but a turnip seed will never attempt to grow into an ear of corn. If you plant a good turnip seed properly a turnip is what you will get every single time.

Any child knows all this, and yet to me it is really impressive to put in row after row of seeds and see them come up without a single mistake. If beets come up in the row you have marked carrots you can be perfectly sure that it is you who have made the error, not the seeds.

Fred and I were married in June of 1929; I was forty-five years old and he was forty-seven. In late summer of that year he asked me if I would like to leave New York City and live in the country. I wasn't unhappy in New York, as some people who love the country are, but I said "yes" without a second's hesitation.

As to that, I don't suppose anyone's happiness is ever seriously affected by his geography. You can't dig your fingers in the fresh warm earth in New York, but there are quite a few things there to enjoy.

Spring comes to New York also. It doesn't bring you crocuses just outside your kitchen door, but it does bring hurdy-gurdies, boys playing marbles, little girls skipping rope. The trees and bushes in Central Park burst out with tender yellow-green leaves just as trees do in the country. And if there is a bird around, it sings, doesn't it?

We all have preferences. I love spring anywhere, but if I could choose I would always greet it in a garden. However, it isn't really important. Spring in the heart on crowded streets with automobile horns shrieking is better, surely, than winter in the heart with daffodils and the call of a redwing.

Fred and I were week-ending with some friends in Connecticut and we told them that we were thinking of moving to the country. They gave us the name of a real-estate agent in Redding Ridge who took us to see a 55-acre farm in Poverty Hollow. Fifty-five acres were many more than we wanted or needed, but the agent said it was quite a bargain and so, more to be obliging than anything else, we went to look at it.

The first thing I spied was a huge lilac bush at the northwest corner of the house. I had been raised on a small farm in Kansas and one of the things that stood out in my memory was the lilac hedge which Mother had planted. When I was thirty-five I realized that I enjoyed hours more than I did dollars and I deliberately achieved, in twenty-four hours, a disregard for material possessions, and had clung to it. Now, suddenly and almost overwhelmingly, I needed to *own* that lilac bush.

Of course, it wasn't in bloom now, in September, but there were only seven months until May. I could wait. Then I remembered that Fred didn't have much money, there were fifty-five acres, and surely he wouldn't buy a place as big as this. So I wandered off and found a lane, lined with apple trees, leading back to the woods. The trees were red with apples; some had fallen to the ground.

Fred called to me to go and look at the house. I went all over it, upstairs and down, and kept saying it was all right, it was fine, or something like that. Actually it was pretty terrible at that time, but my mind was wandering around out of doors.

As soon as I could get away I went back to the lane and ate an apple. I had become used to flabby, anemic, New York City apples and had forgotten that they should be firm, crisp and juicy. This one was a Baldwin; it crackled when I bit into it as though it was having a good time too.

I remembered the Baldwin tree in Kansas, how we didn't know what kind it was and Mother and Dad took some of its apples to a grange meeting and came back and said they were Baldwins. We called the tree "Old Baldy" after that, and this tree looked exactly like Old Baldy.

Fred called me again and tried to get me to take some interest in the house. I went all through it to please him but I couldn't keep my mind on it. This makes me sound a little stupider or at least more impractical and up-in-the-clouds than I actually am. But no doubt you have guessed that I was simply carried back to a happy childhood and had temporarily abandoned the present.

That was true, but there was something else. Living with eight brothers and sisters, even as our number dwindled there had always been someone around who had taken more interest in the house than I had. And always someone with better taste.

I knew that Fred had excellent taste and his word would always be the final one on house arrangement and decoration. That suited me; each to his ability. I could fix up some private nook somewhere the way I liked it. All of my other artistic ideas I would keep to myself since the bulk of them would be courteously but inexorably tabled, and that might hurt my feelings. Whenever possible, I use prevention rather than cure.

When, at 2 o'clock that afternoon, Fred bought the lilac bush and Old Baldy, with a house, barn, and fifty-five acres thrown in, I was almost deliriously happy. Fred had the house done over, making one large living room out of five tiny ones, for instance. He also had the lower floor of the immense barn fitted up with four Spartan bedrooms, kitchen, toilet, washroom, shower and a living room. We furnished it simply but adequately, and printed and mailed an invitation to everyone we knew, telling them to come whenever there was room and stay as long as they pleased. We made it plain that they would have to provide their own food and bed linen and do their own cooking. This included everybody, from family and closest friends to acquaintances of acquaintances.

During that first winter we went out only on week ends. We moved out for keeps on March 28, 1930.

Not very many hours went by before I had a lilac hedge planted along the driveway. I used the shoots that were coming up all around the big bush at the corner of the house. I took a trowel and stuck them into the ground, expecting them to compete with the tough grass which grew all around them. Or, I'm sure, not even giving that a thought.

That was mistake number one. I had not yet heard the warning: "Better a ten-cent rose in a dollar hole than a dollar rose in a ten-cent hole." So I put ten-cent lilac bushes in ten-cent holes and could almost hear myself purring. But the bliss that comes from ignorance should seldom be encouraged for it is likely to do one out of a more satisfying bliss.

Not to be criticized too harshly for this mistake, along with

many others which will follow, perhaps I should tell you that I was only twelve years old when we moved from the farm to Topeka. What little I may have learned about gardening I had completely forgotten.

My two foremost garden advisers, Scott Nearing and my brother Rex, both expert gardeners, should have told me not to have such a big plot plowed up for the vegetables—240 feet by 100 feet. But, perhaps, I wouldn't have listened to them. In those early years I unintelligently planned the garden on this theory: Plant a great deal too much of everything and if only a small percentage comes through you will have enough. One of the results of that crazy idea was that I had, for instance, bushels of cucumbers I couldn't even give away and nothing at all of other, more important things. These were things which required a little knowledge on the part of the gardener, but what time did I have for acquiring knowledge when I was so busy taking care of a garden?

Another mistake: I should have had the plot plowed in the fall. Then the sod would have started to rot. As it was, Ed Carlson, one of my oldest friends, spent many a week end that first summer shaking out sod. Fortunately he enjoyed it and it was a pleasure to watch him. With a summer of sod-shaking ahead he tackled each piece as if it was the last. No problem, no hurry.

In the meantime our ten-year-old niece, Virginia Roddy, who stayed with us every summer from then until she was married, helped me haul away dozens of wheelbarrowsful of stones. Now, they say (I have no way of proving it) that stones are beneficial to the soil. I don't suppose that this means you should leave so many that they are a constant nuisance while you are planting, but I am told now, too late, that Virginia and I hauled away many more thousands of stones than was necessary or even desirable. Don't try to believe that "thousands," if it's a strain, but if I had any way to prove it I'd love to bet a nickel that it's true.

If you plow or spade (I no longer do) you get a new crop

of stones each year. That is, you do if you live in stony Connecticut. It is true, isn't it, that many farmers left Connecticut for the Middle West chiefly or entirely to get away from the stony soil?

One valuable piece of information somehow found its way into my consciousness and stuck. The commonest cause for the failure of seeds to germinate is planting them too deeply. I heeded that warning and, at least, everything came up. What happened next was another story, since I was too busy and too ignorant to care for everything properly.

For instance, I put the turnip seed in in April instead of July. When my mother noticed them in June, she said:

"Ts, ts! 'Twenty-fifth of July, sow turnips wet or dry.' Well, never mind. The tops are good for greens."

Fred didn't like the tops but Virginia and I loved them. That is, I *think* we did; we'd have eaten them even if we had loathed them.

I worked out of doors from daybreak until time to get dinner almost every day. My sister Mary spent a good deal of time in the barn that summer, which was a piece of good luck for Fred since he doesn't care for dust. I mean, Mary kept our house clean and I cooked for her, which suited both of us. And it was fortunate for me that Mother was around a good deal for she took over the flower department.

I happen to be one of those people who are especially fond of flowers. When I worked in New York I sometimes went without lunch and bought myself some flowers instead. However, that is neither as ethereal nor as poverty-stricken as it sounds. I got awfully bored with the restaurants within walking distance of my job and, now and then, roses seemed more appealing than food.

But now with Mother growing every flower in the catalog, and some which I could swear she invented, I concentrated entirely on vegetables. People who didn't know me well got the mistaken impression that I didn't care for flowers.

I found out an interesting thing. You know how some people

seem to think that their love for classical music makes them
spiritual or at least something quite special? And others who
think you are a monster if you don't "love children," however
obnoxious the children may be? Well, I found out that many
people who love flowers look down on those who don't.

I have to admit that I am surprised at those who don't.
There it is: a white, single peony with petals as soft and lustrous
as a butterfly's wing, fragile, graceful. If you touch it you will
find that it is smoother and softer than satin. The fragrance is
so delicate that you must almost hold your breath to get it.

It is a fairy flower. Can you see it, touch it, smell it and
not love it? Amazingly, some people can, but on what grounds
can one feel superior to them for that reason? You can pity them
as you would pity someone who was physically blind and couldn't
see this lovely thing. But how can anyone twist it into a con-
temptuous or superior pity?

Although I couldn't seem to find time to read up on much
of anything, I did try to follow whatever advice came my way.
And so, since Scott had told me that the very latest day for
planting corn in our vicinity was the fifth of July, I marked that
date on the calendar: Corn.

The fifth came and it was pouring rain. I asked Virginia if
she was game to help me put in the last planting of corn. She
was always game and we went out in our shorts and planted
three rows, 240 feet long. I would have been embarrassed if
anyone had asked me what I intended to do with that much corn.

When we got to the house Mother had a pot of hot soup
on the stove for us. She made no comment; she had had nine
children and was used to crazy goings-on. More than that, she
was a Quaker and had the habit of letting everyone follow his
own inner light without any remarks from her.

Cold and wet through, Virginia and I jumped into a tub of
hot water together, ate big bowls of soup and spent the afternoon on the big couch admiring each other's enterprise, which
was more than anyone else did.

That first year I didn't get even one meal of peas. I planted them too late, for one thing. The beets, limas, spinach, lettuce didn't come through. This was probably because the soil was too acid for all except the limas; I found out much later what was wrong with them.

I had had the soil tested by the Farm Bureau and they had told me to put on so-and-so-much lime. Very likely I didn't put on enough for beets, spinach and lettuce, which, I have learned since, need a good deal. Nobody told me either that these things want a generous supply of nitrogen, so I did nothing about that. Like spoiled children, since they didn't get what they wanted, they wouldn't play.

Is anyone curious about how those three rows of corn came out, the ones Virginia and I planted in a driving rain? Well, the crows got some of it. I had never heard of crow repellent. In the bare spots where the corn was missing I put cabbage plants. I was as pleased as a kid when my father, (whose hatred of waste I had either inherited or copied, perhaps) came up one week end and praised me for utilizing the bare spots.

In spite of the crows we had so much corn in late September that it was a problem for anyone who hated waste. So one morning I picked a gross of it (don't you love that, a gross of corn?) and asked Fred to put it in the station wagon and drive me to Danbury to try to sell it.

To Fred's disgust I had refused to learn to drive. I had numerous excellent reasons for not wanting to, but actually only one was necessary: I didn't want to go anywhere.

Fred took me to the general store where we traded, and I told my story. The wife of the man who owned the store bought the corn, put part of it on the sidewalk and stood there by it, calling out to everyone who passed that here was some marvelous corn which had been picked less than an hour ago.

"The woman who grew it picked it herself and brought it in. Just look at it; it don't cost you nothing to look. The woman—"

Everyone was eagerly buying it and I was absurdly proud. Then she spied me sitting in the station wagon waiting for Fred, got excited, pointed at me and cried: "Look at her! There she sits now. She picked this marvelous corn only one hour ago, not even. There she sits. Just look at her!"

They looked, naturally, and naturally I was embarrassed.

As a child I had a lively imagination and lofty ambitions. I thought up many remarkable things I would do some day which would make people stare at me, nudge each other and whisper: "There she is. Look at her!"

I was sure I had covered everything then but it hadn't occurred to me once to include picking corn.

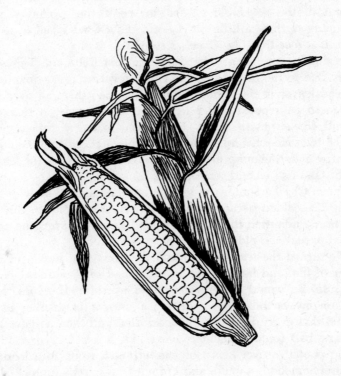

The Second Season

ON THOSE BRILLIANT and, at the same time, mellow days which we get once in awhile in February, when the sun is so warm that it seems to ignore your clothes and touch your skin, I would go out to the vegetable garden to see if the ground wasn't beginning to thaw a little bit. I don't know what I had in mind to do if it *was* thawing. Cheer, I suppose.

It didn't even begin to get soft, that first February. This was partly due to the fact that I had raked together great quantities of dead leaves in the autumn and had spread them all over the garden to be plowed under in the spring. If you do that the ground freezes more slowly but, once frozen, it thaws more slowly too. No one told me to do this but, since I couldn't afford as much manure as I would have liked, I thought leaves would take its place to some extent.

When Charlie Stauffer, a near-by farmer, came to plow in the spring he scolded because the leaves were troublesome. But he reluctantly admitted that it was a good thing for everyone concerned except the plowman.

He turned the leaves under and then his good heart got the better of him and he sold me an extra load of manure which, I feel sure, he would have preferred to use himself. More than that, on my birthday he made me a present of another load. He did that every June until his cow died and then he gave me the cow bell for a memento.

No poet I've ever heard of has written an ode to a load of manure. Somebody should, and I'm not trying to be funny.

You take your pitchfork and lift off a big hunk of the rich, gorgeous, smelly stuff and bring to light a colony of earthworms. It would be difficult to think up anything more repulsive-looking than a lot of earthworms wriggling around in moist manure. I can remember the time when I would have thought I owed it to my fastidiousness to be nauseated at the sight.

No longer. My respect for their role in the scheme of things overshadows my distaste. I don't know just what a poet could say to a fine pile of manure, but to an earthworm he might say: "Little repulsive object, no doubt you think it is unjust that useless things are often beautiful. Unfair that we exclaim with rapture over a splendid sunset or a blue lobelia while we squeamishly turn away from you. But don't be greedy, little creature. We need you more than we need flaming sunset or sweet lilac or graceful deer. Must you have beauty also?"

That might comfort him. On the other hand, it is possible that he does not give a hoot that we are repelled by him. For all we know, he may even be a sadist and enjoy giving us the shivers.

While it lasted, my devotion to manure was well known. One Easter Sunday two of my young friends showed up with gifts. Cal Kallgren came first with a lovely yellow rose. A few hours later Bob Allen drove in with a load of manure. It would be difficult to say which pleased me more, each so different but both so desirable.

One more story, then we'll get back on the job. One week end Fred and I went to Long Island. Our hostess asked several mutual friends in for the evening. Some of them were interested in gardening, so you can imagine what happened.

I was all decked out in a fresh permanent, a long dinner dress, and my handsomest earrings. Finally someone could stand it no longer and exclaimed: "For pity's sake, can't somebody stop her? She looks like a glamour girl and can't talk about a thing but manure."

To get back to Charlie, I think the most valuable thing he taught me was how to protect newly planted corn from the crows. He mixed a few spoonfuls of arsenate of lead in enough water to make a milky liquid and wet the corn seed thoroughly with it. I don't believe I have ever come across anybody who knows about this, while a number of people have told me that crow repellent doesn't always repel.

I usually treated my seed in the winter as soon as it arrived, spread it out on papers to dry and then put it back into the envelopes. It is easier to plant dry than wet. I have now graduated from using any kind of poison in the garden and have had to evolve another system for defeating the crows.

Another thing Charlie told me that second summer, which you may not know if you are a beginner, was this: If your tomato plants are tall ones when you put them in the ground make a trench about four inches deep and almost as long as each plant. Lay the tomato plant in the trench and bury all of it except about eight inches of the top. Press the soil down firmly. The top will just lie there on the ground. Leave it alone; it will get up when it feels like it. Or rather, the sun will attract it and it will rise to meet it.

As I understand it, there are two reasons for doing this. One, the plant makes roots all along the stem and therefore becomes stronger. Two, a newly transplanted thing is better off not to be tall and unsteady and shouldn't have many leaves exposed to sun and wind.

The lilac hedge I had put in a year ago was between the house and the vegetable garden, which meant that I saw it several times a day. This was unfortunate, for you can scarcely imagine a more depressing sight. As I told you, I had stuck the little, defenseless things into holes barely big enough to hold them, expecting them to cope with the energetic grass roots crowding up against them.

This second spring they seemed to be somewhat smaller than they were when I put them there. To call them a hedge, even just in my mind and while thinking of their future growth, was laughable, in a melancholy way. I didn't ask myself or anybody else the reason for their arrested development. I was intent on activities about to be started or in the process; the hedge was

a finished project. I had done my part, what more did they want?
What were they waiting for?

My biggest job that spring in terms of long hours of hard
labor was the asparagus bed. As I think back on it now it seems
most unlikely that I am telling the truth, yet I know that I am.

I, personally, dug two trenches the entire length of the
garden (240 feet) and they were two feet deep and 22 inches
wide. Then, still personally, I filled up the trenches to within
a few inches of the top with a combination of dirt and manure,
mixing the two together thoroughly with a spading fork. Unless
you work with a road gang you won't realize what a job this was.

I then planted two-year-old asparagus roots in this mon-
strosity. I call it that because I found out later all that work
was unnecessary. I hasten to add, however, that I didn't make
up this method. In those days this was what experts told you
to do. I doubt very much if any expert ever did it himself.

I am not the type of woman who can lay stone fences, paint
houses, and wield a hammer effectively. I win (when I win)
through stubborn persistence and endurance, rather than through
physical prowess. Therefore I suppose it is time for me to explain
why Fred didn't do any of this manual labor.

This second season he was writing a book and digging a
lily- and frog pond in the yard. We had an understanding that
we would each do exactly what we wanted to do around the
place and neither of us would expect the other to help (or
interfere) with his particular program. I knew perfectly well
that he wished I would content myself with a doll-size vegetable
garden, play croquet and sit under a maple tree and read or
write a book. But he kept still about his wishes.

He hardly ever went out to visit the vegetable garden. It
is true that he wasn't interested, but I imagine he avoided it
chiefly because, like everyone else, he was pretty sure I was
killing myself out there and didn't want to catch me at it for
fear he couldn't stop me. He would have put his foot down and

hired a man to dig those trenches if he had had any notion of how hard I was working. That was why I did the job piecemeal, filling up the trenches as I went along, so that a layman, like Fred, wouldn't catch on to the magnitude of the enterprise.

I seemed to have a mania for doing everything myself if I possibly could. Throughout my life I had heard my mother often say: "What would we ever do without the men in this world?" But, oftener: "If you want anything done, do it yourself." The second one seemed to have taken root.

Also, these were the early depression years; money was scarce. But, chiefly, I wanted no one lifting a finger in that garden unless he loved doing it. What if Fred had hired a man to dig those trenches and it had turned out that he didn't love to dig? Who could eat that kind of asparagus?

I at once bought a tool for cutting the crop although I knew I must not harvest any the first year. The second year you may cut it for a week; after that for six weeks. Some people say that a bed, properly cared for, will last forever; others will tell you that it will eventually peter out. Ours is twenty-four years old and is still behaving itself. Of course, that is not forever. I only hope that it will last as long as we do, for that is one vegetable which Fred will eat gladly every day as long as it is in season.

Gathering asparagus was tedious work. You had to push the tool into the ground close to a stalk and cut the asparagus an inch or two beneath the surface of the earth. This meant that not only the bottom of each stalk was dirty, but also two or more inches of it were tough and had to be cut off. It took time, for you had to be careful not to injure a near by stalk which had not yet come up above the surface of the ground.

After a few years of going through that cumbersome procedure I cheated when I was in a hurry and, instead of using the tool, went quickly down the row and snapped off each stalk wherever it broke easily. This took about one-tenth the time and saved a lot of minutes in the kitchen, too. No dirty, tough ends to cut off and dispose of.

I was a little afraid that doing this might be harmful to the bed, although I couldn't figure out any reason why it should be. Therefore, when I wasn't in much of a hurry I still took my tool and did it the "right" way. After several years of this I read an article: Great discovery! The way to pick asparagus was to break it off where it was tender.

I didn't throw away the tool, although I never used it again for cutting asparagus. It is almost the handiest one I have, perfect for digging dandelions, burdock, or any other deep-rooted perennial weeds. Fine, too, for digging carrots.

It was some years later that I learned that I need not have dug those trenches. It wasn't necessary to go down all the way to China. Just dig a shallow trench, toss in some manure and dirt and plant your roots.

I wasted no time in indignation or regret. By then I was a full-fledged farmer: philosophical. I merely shrugged my shoulders. What did it matter? What would be better in my life now if I had done something else instead of digging those trenches?

That second summer we met John Lorenz. Through the years he has become my number-one adviser. Although our gardens are a mile apart you could almost say we have one garden. If either of us has a surplus of anything, the other is the one to get it if he wants it. Much more than that, if I had only two heads of cauliflower and John had none, he'd get one of mine. And he does the same for me.

He told me the first day I met him that I was planting most things too early.

"Prove it for yourself," he said. "Plant some carrots and beets the first of April and another row the first of May. Even if May doesn't exactly catch up with April, they'll turn out better because they haven't been shivering the pep out of them for a month. They'll grow quicker, and anything is better if it grows fast."

He was right; he is always right because he doesn't speak up unless he knows. I did my best to restrain myself after that, but you have to be well supplied with will power and self-discipline to keep yourself from scattering every seed you can lay your hands on when one of those summer days in April comes along.

That second year we had about two or three scanty meals of peas from a 240-foot row. No lettuce. About five little beets.

I planted New Zealand spinach because I hadn't any luck with the other kind and I was told this was perennial. Fred and Mary didn't care much for it, so I pulled it up. And yet, with all the failures, there was always some fresh vegetable for the table. Keeping the expense of food down to a minimum became a matter of great pride to me.

But Fred liked meat. One evening at dinner the only things which had come out of a store were coffee and a small amount of meat in the stuffed peppers. I got the feeling that Fred wasn't enjoying the menu as thoroughly as could be desired, so I said enthusiastically: "This whole dinner cost only about thirty cents."

Fred answered: "Good for you. But now I'm going to make a trip to the refrigerator and that's going to run into real money."

I got up at six o'clock every morning (five by standard time) and neither needed the pity nor deserved the admiration that I got for it because I've always liked to get up when the sun does.

Why do people who like to get up early look with disdain on those who like to lie in bed late? And why do people who like to work feel superior to those who prefer to dream?

Some of the nicest people I know would rather lie on the grass and watch fat, white clouds languidly play tag with each other in a deep-blue sky than dig an asparagus trench. Maybe they are just plain lazy or maybe they are poets, by temperament if not by performance. In either case, why disturb them? It seems to me that our first obligation to ourselves, our family and friends, and to society, is to be happy. If they are happy lying on the grass they are only doing their duty.

I would like to get lyrical on the subject of 5 A.M. in a garden, but it is not the paradise it should be, especially in early spring. The air is invigorating and at its freshest; the solitude is divine. The birds are happy, but, unfortunately, so are the gnats. The early bird may get the worm but the early gnat gets me. The dew is a lovely thing to look at sparkling on the grass, but a nuisance in the garden.

Very early morning in New York City is by far the best time of day. It is relatively quiet and the air is, of course, at its rather poor best. It is exclusive; there is only one class of people abroad at that hour—the lowly workers. No shoppers, no idle strollers, no executives—no one to whom anybody has to say "sir" or "ma'am." It is intimate: If you call "good morning" to a garbage collector, a shoe black or someone sweeping the sidewalk he'll respond without thinking you are either mistaken or insane, as he would think later in the day.

If you have been out all night at a party and are returning early in the morning, don't imagine that you can get the spirit of this fresh, friendly hour. You are an outsider and everybody knows it. You don't belong. In any field of life the observer can never experience the feel of the kernel of a thing as the partaker does. In my opinion that is why rich people lead such pitifully barren lives. They are completely shut off from the primary motif of existence, the scramble to find a way to stay alive.

One bright, unusually chilly morning in late May I didn't go out to the vegetable garden until after breakfast because we had been to a dinner party the night before and had come home after midnight.

Everything was in its proper place, looking contented and hearty, until I reached the tomato plants, four dozen of them. They were black and limp. For a moment I had no idea what was wrong with them and then I realized. Frozen. Dead.

I don't know how long I stood there. After awhile I turned and walked slowly back to the house. Fred was in the yard.

"What's the matter?" he asked.

"The tomatoes are frozen."

He put his arm around my shoulders.

"It's not a major calamity," he said sympathetically. "I'll drive you down to Mead's right away and get some more. I'll help you plant them. It's not worth crying about. Don't cry."

"Who's going to cry?" I began indignantly, but I put my hand up to my face and realized then that tears were actually brimming over.

Yes, I know, I feel just the way you do about a grown woman who cries over a broken cup, no matter how beautiful and old and rare it is, no matter, even, who gave it to her. But a cup has fulfilled its destiny; it will never be anything more than it has already been. While a young tomato plant is full of plans. It expects to grow and bear fruit and feed people. Let the frost kill it in October. It has outlived its usefulness and beauty then. It has done its job.

That afternoon we bought more tomato plants, and after forty-eight hours I had almost forgotten the forty-eight little tragedies. But the shock of untimely death of flowers and fruit and vegetables (and I have had many such shocks in the last twenty-five years) is never softened by repetition. Death of the old is merely sad, but death of the young is outrageous.

It's the Struggle That Counts

Is THERE ANY SENSE to the notion that a person has to know a subject from A to Z in order to begin teaching it effectively? If you are sure of your ground as far as you have gone, if you know the alphabet up to M, let us say, you can teach that much of it, can't you?

Years ago I horrified my piano teacher by giving lessons to my nephew and niece, Roger and Juanita, after I had had my first lesson. I patiently explained to her that if I knew where C was and if I could play a scale I could certainly tell the children about it. Show them when to start with the thumb the second time. That's what teaching is, isn't it, telling and showing something you know to somebody else?

Following up that theory, in my third year of gardening I began to teach it. Next to working in my own garden I liked starting one for somebody else.

Fortunately, I didn't have many pupils since each one took quite a lot of time. They would call for me in the morning, I would work with them all day and Fred would come over late in the afternoon and we'd all have dinner together.

Last spring when we went to visit the Pecks, Sterling pointed to some peonies, a long border of daffodils, great clusters of grape hyacinths and said: "You did that, Ruth, twenty-two years ago."

It gave me a good feeling. But for me, where would all that beauty be now? I was always at a loss in my friends' kitchens (to say nothing of my own) and so it was especially pleasant to be of some use in their gardens.

Although I had never planted any for us, I put a row of potatoes in for a sick neighbor. When I told Mary, she persuaded me to grow a few for us because it was so much fun to dig them. That may sound absurd if you have never done it, but it is fascinating to put your spading fork in the ground and, instead of turning over a forkful of dirt, see a lot of potatoes rolling out of the earth. It's like finding an unexpected treasure.

Through the years I have grown them only three or four times; we don't eat enough of them to make it worth while. But I intend to plant some again one of these days because somebody (I think it was Scott) told me of an easy way to do it. He makes a furrow, drops in his pieces of seed potato and tosses hay on them. When the tops die down he rakes off the hay and there are his new potatoes, clean and waiting to be picked up instead of dug. Of course that system is worthless if you plant potatoes primarily for the fun of digging them, but few people do.

I gave lots of vegetables to the barn guests; the garden was a boon to them. And it was a real life saver for us when unexpected guests arrived conveniently (for them) at mealtime.

On Labor Day that third summer eighteen of such guests drove in. Most of them were on their way back to New York after the holiday. Mary, with Virginia and her brother Roger, went out to the corn belt five different times as car after car appeared.

Without even knowing it I was an inadequate cook in the early years of my marriage. If I had tried to get a regular dinner that day there is no question about it, it would have been a highly inferior meal. But Mary and Virginia were expert corn pickers and, by steaming it for five minutes instead of boiling it, even I couldn't hurt properly picked corn, fresh from the patch. Those of the guests who weren't glad they were eating corn and tomatoes that day instead of steak or chicken didn't know all the ins and outs of the culinary department.

Scattered hither and yon over the fifty-five acres were hundreds of blueberry bushes. Virginia and I picked many gallons of berries that summer. No, I don't mean quarts. Mary sat in the yard under, a tree and cleaned them, hour after hour. She preferred to do that and Virginia and I preferred to pick.

Since not one of us was particularly fond of blueberries this was, not to put it too unkindly, a rather peculiar enterprise. But the bushes were tall and easy to pick from, the berries hung in great clusters, they were large and tempting, and how could anybody just leave them there?

Mary maintained that she liked them cooked but when it came to the crucial test she didn't do much to substantiate her claim. I am fond of cream, so I ate some now and then when I couldn't find anything else to put cream on. Fred said he loved blueberry pie, a dish which was missing in my repertoire. When my sister Elizabeth came out for a few days she made him a blueberry pie, but it turned out that he had meant blackberry.

Virginia made no pretense of liking them in any form. And the barn guests were no help at all; they insisted on picking their own.

Nadya Thomas, a Russian girl I had met when I was in Russia with a Quaker famine-relief group, had married an American and was living in New York. She came to spend a few weeks in the barn and persuaded me to can the surplus blueberries.

We cooked on an oil stove in those days and she and I canned thirty-six quarts of berries by the hot-water method. If you don't think that was a horrible job you are quite mistaken.

She took half of them home with her; I kept half and they came in handy. We had a great many week-end guests in the house in the winter time and a lot of people seem to like blueberries.

Unfortunately, the following summer provided another bumper crop. Nadya wasn't there but Virginia and I again picked gallons. Mary cleaned them and we all three set out to can them.

It isn't likely that you will guess what happened next. Just before the final operation, whatever that was (thank the Lord I don't remember), I announced: "I'm not going to can a single berry."

Mary and Virgina were aghast.

"But—we already have."

"Not yet. Not quite. If we finish them, all I'll remember next summer is how nice it was to have them through the winter. I'll completely forget this ghastly business, or at least I'll minimize it. The only way I'll learn is to quit right now."

We quit. Jake Baker was there and he persuaded us to strain the stuff and make juice. It would last quite a while in the refrigerator, he said. So we did that and it was pretty good.

Everyone who heard that story thought I was crazy. I think it was one of the most intelligent things I've ever done. It worked.

Virginia and I were never able, however, to stop picking blueberries. We made juice out of them, gave some away, and, finally, softhearted Dominick, the fruit and vegetable man who came to the door twice a week, took pity on us and bought a good many at some low price.

My indifference to blueberries somehow reminded me that I was especially fond of raspberries, so I ordered some bushes that winter to be planted the following spring. While we are at it, we may as well go on with the raspberry tale up to the present time.

I put a 240-foot row of them down the garden, outside the asparagus. We barely got enough to eat until a few years later when Fred turned half of the barn into a shop where he made wooden bowls, plates and so on. The sawdust had to be disposed of; I couldn't seem to keep the weeds out of the raspberry patch, so I dumped the sawdust all around the bushes. Kill or cure, I thought. It was miraculous. As long as I kept that up we had so many raspberries that keeping them picked was a problem.

When, later, I reduced the size of the garden I abandoned that row of berries. Charlie Stauffer gave me some black raspberry roots which I grew for a few years. They let their branches droop and touch the ground and make new roots at the tip of each branch unless you keep them clipped back. I decided this was too haphazard and took up too much room, but I think I was just making excuses to get rid of them. The real trouble

was that they were much thornier than the red kind and, whenever feasible, I avoided thorns. So I threw out the black ones
and went back to the red.

I now have only eight bushes of those, plenty for eating,
freezing and jam, because they are mulched with sawdust and
wood chips. That is the answer for raspberries. I wish you could
see Scott's bushes in Vermont, thriving under the sawdust routine.

By degrees and in a spotty way the garden was improving.
Now, of course, I was planting turnips in July and had some fine
white ones. But the rutabagas didn't do a thing for me. They
just sat there, reproaching me, I suppose, because I never got
around to thinning them. It wasn't only a matter of time; I
didn't realize then how set in their way rutabagas are. They
simply will not budge if you don't thin them. Other root vegetables aren't that stubborn. Carrots, beets and white turnips
won't do their best without being thinned, but they will do
something.

I may have got my aversion to thinning from Mother. She
would plant a row of flower seeds, and if you asked her if they
shouldn't be thinned, she would answer: "Yes, of course they
should. I'll go in the house and you do it if you can bear to."
She probably meant: If you are that high principled and strong
and cruel.

Whatever you do about thinning, it is painful. If you pull
out dozens of little growing plants and throw them away you
feel like a minor murderer. But if you don't do that, if you plant
some seeds and then, after they come up, you let them all waste
their lives through your inability to destroy enough of them to
give the rest a chance to grow up and amount to something, that
is a sin against all of them. Then you feel like a parent who
hasn't the strength of character to hurt in order to help.

During these first years, cultivating was the job I liked best.
Take a bright sunny morning after a good night's rain, a hoe or
long-handled cultivator, and row upon row of young and ambi-
tious vegetables, with millions of tiny weeds starting or planning-
to start to thwart them. What an exhilarating job it is to foil

the enemies and save those little fellows which have such a high purpose in mind: feeding and nourishing you!

That third summer it rained often, and one of the things I had heard and was trying to follow was that you should cultivate a garden after every rain. This was a job with a garden the size of mine when it rained two or three times a week. Sometimes I would get so tired doing the same motion hour after hour that I would take a rake and drag it behind me between the rows that were planted three feet apart, such as corn and the cabbage family. That was far from satisfactory because I couldn't look at the splendid improvement as I went along, which was half of the pleasure of cultivating. However, it may have been just as well that I couldn't see what I was doing. Pulling a rake behind you is not the most effective way of cultivating.

One afternoon that summer we went to visit Jim and Winifred Rorty. Of course I wanted to see their vegetable garden. I was shocked. The whole garden was so choked with weeds that you could hardly see what was growing there.

Jim didn't seem to be ashamed in the least. He bent over and pulled up a good-sized beet.

"But," I protested, "I haven't got a weed in my beets. And you ought to see them. But you'd need a microscope."

"Luck," Jim said generously. "Evidently my soil is so rich and so right for these things that this season at least they come through in spite of weeds. I can't get away with it forever."

He pulled up several beets and gave them to me. I hope I thanked him—oh, I'm sure I must have. But I didn't feel grateful; I didn't want his beets. I wanted my own.

Our driveway, which is about twenty feet from the house, was a public road. Nobody ever used it, but any day people might begin building on the land beyond us leading to Newtown. I can imagine no one so bored or lonely that he would welcome the thought of his driveway turning into a public thoroughfare. We felt uneasy about it.

Therefore, when the town wanted to buy some gravel from

us, Fred arranged for them to pay for it by building a cut-off some two or three hundred yards from the house, to meet the road further up. When it was completed we deeded it to the town in exchange for the piece near our house.

What has this got to do with gardening? More than you would ever dream.

While the men were working on the job we asked them to dispose of the topsoil by dumping it onto the vegetable garden, which was quite handy for them. They did it willingly. When they were finished and Fred went out to look at it he could hardly bear to tell me the bitter news.

The "topsoil" was practically nothing but sand and stones, of which that poor garden had already had far more than its quota. The endless work I had gone to in order to bring down the percentage of sand! Much worse than that, those men, wanting to be nice to us or at least having nothing against us, for some unaccountable reason had run their tremendous roller over the "topsoil." We couldn't figure out why on earth they had done such a thing unless they had become so accustomed to building roads that they couldn't break the habit.

We didn't know which would be the least bad thing to do now: plow up some sod for a new garden patch somewhere else or have this distressing thing plowed. The former would have meant struggling again with sod, and Ed Carlson, helper number one in that department, had gone home to Colorado. Also, the new garden would be farther from the house, which is a disadvantage. Even if you are methodical and try to pick everything you need at one time, you can hardly escape extra trips for a few radishes, scallions, some parsley, a bit of dill. Also, the asparagus bed which, thank goodness, had escaped their ministrations, would then be a separate unit. That would be undesirable, for it would be then entirely surrounded by encroaching grass, which it wasn't now, with other vegetables adjoining one long side of it. Added to all this, if we moved to another spot we would lose all the valuable soil I had begun to build here with leaves and manure.

We didn't know what might be the drawbacks to plowing up this hard bit of pavement, so I wrote to the state agricultural college at Storrs to ask their advice. They sent a man to look over the situation. He said to go on with the old garden if I had the courage to face it, and added that in the long run the whole thing would turn out to be an advantage. I am still trying to figure out what he meant by that because, honestly, those men had added almost nothing but more stones and gravel.

If I had grasped the opportunity it could have been advantageous as a character builder. For this would have been the perfect time to reduce the size of the garden. But I am the kind of person who thinks up a snappy answer the next morning. I thought of having only half the garden plowed after Charlie, in an aura of groans and swear words, had plowed it all.

I wrote to Virginia and broke the bad news: a few additional stones to cart away. She didn't wait until school was out in June to come to the rescue, but persuaded her father to drive her up for a few week ends to give me a hand. Sometimes she brought two or three friends along and they all pitched in. Fred said he was going to report me for employing child labor. Virginia's answer to that was: "What do you mean—*employ?*"

I have no way of knowing whether or not the Storrs man was right. I have a fine garden now, but I seriously doubt that that excellent paving job had anything to do with it. On the other hand, probably the bad feaures of it were only temporary: the work of hauling away the boulders, as Virginia called them, and difficulty in plowing that spring. It did seem to me that the soil was much poorer for a year or two, but that may have been only because I had expected it to be.

Farmers are philosophical; they have learned that it is less wearing to shrug their shoulders than to beat their breasts. But there is another angle to their attitude. Things happen rapidly in the country; something new always comes along to divert them and it isn't necessarily another calamity.

For instance, when despair over the paved garden was at its peak, crocuses, yellow, white and lavender, serenely smiled at me. Wise little pacifists! Harsh winds, cutting sleet, drifting snow—nothing tempts them to destroy themselves by fighting back. They wait, and when the violence wears itself out, they open wide eyes and turn to the sun.

However, you can be comforted by a crocus just so long. You are bound to return to your misery. But then April dances in, calling "April Fool!" to you wherever you turn. None of the dead-looking things were dead, merely sleeping, taking a much-needed rest. April Fool! Daffodils, lilacs, tulips, peonies, roses, even the grass, are all coming back to life. What more do you want?

Well, of course you want a vegetable garden, too. But there is no denying that all these live, growing things divert and excite you and do everything possible to keep you from jumping in the well to drown your troubles.

Again I had no luck with beets, lettuce, spinach and peas. For one thing it was quite impossible to get the garden plowed early enough for the things that liked cool weather. It is my experience that all plows automatically break down sometime in March and stay that way until late in April. Also I'm pretty sure that the lettuce, spinach and beets needed more lime and nitrogen.

However, I had little time to worry about the failures. I was so busy picking and trying to get rid of string beans, tomatoes, bushels of cucumbers and hundreds of ears of corn that I had little interest in what wasn't there.

I could have grown Swiss chard instead of spinach, but Fred and Virginia didn't like it. Lettuce bored Fred. Mary liked beets and I was sorry they didn't do better, but too occupied to do anything more about it than feel sorry.

Peas were the one failure that really bothered me. We all liked them and I was willing to spend some time in learning how to grow them successfully. I complained to Scott about it; he saved seed from his own peas and said he would send me some.

I remembered that he grew the tall kind and said I couldn't face cutting and placing brush for 240 feet of peas.

"Why must you have 240 feet?" he asked.

I didn't know the answer to that, so I changed the subject. Before he left Scott came back to it.

"Don't order any peas," he said. "I'll send you some. Plant them and don't worry about the brush."

He sent me three pounds of seed and I planted it, thinking—well, not thinking, I guess, not trying to figure out what magic Scott had used to keep them from needing brush. He said not to worry and he never used idle words.

The peas grew until they were about six inches high. One afternoon I looked out of the window and saw a man bending over doing something in the vegetable garden. No man except John could do so much as pull a weed out there without making me nervous ever since Hal Hirsch had weeded the radishes to surprise me and had pulled up the radishes instead of the weeds.

I knew that wasn't John out there now, so I went to investigate. It was Scott. He was brushing the peas with branches he had cut and brought all the way down from Vermont in his truck.

I wasn't surprised. It was typical of him to do a wonderful thing like that, typical, too, to go straight to the garden and do the job before even coming in to greet us.

But the story has an unsatisfactory ending: we didn't get many peas. And that year I had got them in early by digging a shallow trench adjoining the asparagus and putting in the seed before the plot was plowed. I had got them in by the first of April, yet it was a poor crop.

I had been told that Connecticut was far from ideal for growing peas. The local farmers and gardeners said they seldom got enough to can. I was tempted to give up and might have if the build-up for Lincoln peas in Joseph Harris's catalog had not tempted me to try once more. I had found that you didn't go wrong if you followed their advice about what to plant, for either quality or quantity. So I put in Lincoln, and that year we had more peas than we could eat. Later, when I began to preserve my vegetables, we had peas all winter.

When some of the local women asked me what I did in order to have peas to can, I told them I had never had half enough to eat, let alone preserve, until I grew Lincoln. They were too polite to argue the point, but obviously they didn't believe the variety had anything to do with my success for they stuck to whatever kind they had been growing. However, as through the years I picked peas by the bushel while they picked them by the quart, they gave in, one by one, planted Lincoln peas and began to can them.

I don't know why this is so. Of course many people grow other varieties with success. However, the above has been not only my experience but that of a dozen or more neighbors and friends in this locality.

John was one of the hardest to convince, but now he wouldn't grow any other kind. Many years later when I met Bob Allen, an inexperienced but highly intelligent and enthusiastic gardener, at first he laughed at my devotion to Lincoln but grew a few to humor me. Before two seasons went by he abandoned all other varieties, although he would have greatly preferred to pick the tall growing ones.

It didn't take me long to find out that starting such things as tomatoes and peppers from seed was not my talent. I bought my plants from Frank Mead, a pleasant, obliging fellow who works in a hat factory and takes care of his hothouse in his spare time. He and I became friendly enough for me to dare to ask him if he would grow some Vinedale pepper plants for me. Carl Warren, of Joseph Harris, told me that these would ripen even in our short season. I found that they did. And, incidentally, no one has been of more help to me with garden advice than Carl Warren.

Many people, including some gardeners, don't know that sweet green peppers turn red when they are ripe, just as a tomato does. They think that all red peppers are hot. But all peppers will turn red if you let them, and the nutritionists say that they are more valuable in vitamins when they are ripe. They taste better, too, sweeter and milder.

One year I bought some ground cherry tomato seed which Mr. Mead started for me. These are not a true tomato. The plant looks so unlike a tomato plant that one day when Mary and I were weeding she began pulling out the ground cherry plants. And she is no amateur.

The fruit is small and round, similar to a red cherry tomato (or a red cherry, for that matter); it is yellow and sweet like a sweet fruit; the flavor has no relation to that of a tomato.

After several years of staking and pruning tomato plants I discarded that method and bought salt hay, which I spread on the ground, letting the plants roam at will on this fine, clean bed. I envied them, doing their work lying down. This method takes more space and less time than tying the plants to stakes; I was long on space and short on time.

If you prune tomatoes, sometimes in hot, dry weather there are not enough leaves to protect them from the merciless sun. Then the fruit will get a large, whitish inedible spot on one side. Even if you don't prune them the sun may burn them. If they are not staked it is easy enough to toss a little hay on those that are exposed.

It is surprising how many seasoned gardeners don't know that it is the leaf of the plant that needs the sun, not the fruit. Tomatoes, strawberries, melons will grow and ripen perfectly and have the finest flavor possible without the sun ever touching the fruit itself. I think it was Rex who told me that fruit is even better off without direct sun on it, and I believe he said that some growers of fine grapes cover the bunches of grapes for that reason.

That seems like quite a job; surely somebody will invent a gadget to take care of it. Press a button at the proper moment and little paper bags will pop out from nowhere and fit themselves neatly around the bunches of grapes.

I am not against gadgets. I have a contraption on the kitchen wall for opening various kinds of jars and bottles and it requires neither brains nor skill with the fingers. I would hate to part with it. And I would rather turn on the light at the head of the couch with a flip of the switch than to fill and clean a kerosene lamp. Trimming the wicks and washing the lamp chimneys was my job when I was a little girl, and I know what I'm talking about.

In the garden, though, I still like to use my brains. I am glad there is no chance of my living until that time when people can sit in an armchair and press one button for rain, another for sun, a third for nitrogen, a fourth for humus and a fifth for the desired temperature.

In some far day, when we have learned to use our minds for greater things, this button-pushing will come in handy. In the meantime, it is the fight against big odds which puts iron into our souls, forcing us to accept the bitter as well as the sweet. If we can learn to do this cheerfully and accept victory with humility, defeat with serenity, we are moving forward.

Waste Not, Want Not

To THOSE OF YOU who have moved from the city to the country and have undertaken gardening, building, landscaping, remodeling, this account of my first years of gardening will not seem overdrawn. Most people in these circumstances seem to become overenthusiastic, attempt too much and make many mistakes. I have gone into detail about it primarily for the sake of those who are in the early stages of this adventure and are looking forward to having a garden.

When the farmers around here take leave of you their parting words are almost never "Goodby" or "So long," but "Take it easy." Several years passed before I learned to follow this sensible advice; I hope you will be more open to it than I was.

Until I was twelve years old we lived on a farm in Kansas, and there was nothing hectic about it. My father was superintendent of schools and my grandfather was in charge of the farming. After school hours and through the summer the older boys, Bob and Walt, were his assistants.

Grandpa was slow-moving and gentle; no doubt he worked steadily, but he didn't overdo it and he never hurried. The boys liked to lie under an apple tree and read Jesse James and pay Rex, the little fellow, a nickel to hoe a row of corn and a penny to tell them if he saw Dad or Grandpa coming.

It was an easy-going farm and yet we had plenty of fine corn and Dad sold sweet potatoes, strawberries, muskmelons and watermelons.

It may be that these early happy years gave me my great

love for the soil, although I doubt it. I think I would have learned
to love it, given the chance to get my fingers into it, no matter
where I was brought up.

You can, if you have sufficient will power, force yourself
not to attempt more than you can do comfortably, but I'm
afraid you may as well resign yourself to making some mistakes.
Nobody can tell you everything all at once, and books and
magazine articles often seem vague to the beginner. Unless you
are lucky, you will run into two articles about the same thing
which contradict each other. Armchair gardeners mean well,
I'm sure, but they have a bad habit of confusing surmise with
fact.

This makes you realize that the very last word about growing
things has not been said, any more than it has been about
medicine, nutrition, and quite a few other things. Fortunately,
there is no law against your doing a bit of experimenting on
your own.

And so in winter I would try to figure out shortcuts. I was
not good at putting in bean poles, never got them deep enough,
and was ever on the lookout for some magic formula which
would simplify this job for me.

One winter I noticed Russian sunflowers in the catalog; they
were supposed to grow to be exceptionally tall. They had a
double sentimental and nostalgic appeal for me: Kansas was
the Sunflower State and, ten years back, when I spent a year in
Russia, I had fallen in love with the Russian peasants, who
taught me to enjoy eating sunflower seeds.

There should be some affinity between Russian sunflowers
and me. Why wouldn't they be glad to make effective bean
poles for me?

I sent for a package of seeds and planted a few where I
wanted the bean poles. A little later I planted beans around them
and, sure enough, it worked.

I pulled out all of the little sunflower plants except one in
each hill, and that one grew tall and straight and strong and the
bean vines climbed up on it. It was beginner's luck, however.

The two following years, for some reason or other, the sunflowers didn't make a good, strong growth.

Next I tried planting corn to use for poles. This worked fairly well for a year or two, but then for a couple of seasons the corn wouldn't grow fast enough to support the beans adequately. Now I have gone back to regular poles, but I am sure if I took the trouble (and it wouldn't be *much* trouble) to start corn or sunflowers under hotkaps (waxed paper cones) I would be successful. Let the stalks get a head start so the beans won't be asking for support before they are competent to give it.

Next spring I am going to do all three: sunflowers, corn and regular poles.

I tried another experiment: I stopped "suckering" corn, to find out if it was necessary. For beginners I will explain that a sucker is the shoot that grows at the bottom of a stalk of corn. Usually there are more than one to each stalk and they are supposed to take some strength away from the main stalk. But suckering corn took the strength out of me, and I asked myself which was more important—me or the corn? Wishing to be fair, I compromised, suckered half of it and left the other half alone. As near as I could tell they both came out the same. The pun, of course, inevitably followed: If you are a sucker, sucker corn.

And now the authorities tell you not to do it.

It is only natural that by degrees you begin to read the authorities with a raised eyebrow, but of course it would be far from safe to ignore them completely. For instance, they tell you (and you find out that it is true) that string beans do well in poor soil; that the soil for peppers must not be too rich or you will get big plants without any peppers; that all members of the cabbage family are gross feeders.

When I read this I was as kind to the greedy cabbage and cauliflower as I felt I could afford to be, which was not very kind. The bulk of the manure went to strawberries, asparagus, roses, peonies and peas. What little I could spare after that I usually tucked around some hills of corn. No book had told me to do that, but I had such a high regard for both corn and manure I didn't see how they could fail to want to be together.

Here is a mistake I want to warn you against. Everyone will tell you that there is nothing to growing rhubarb, but don't let that fool you.

It gave me the impression that all you needed to do was plant the roots and pick the rhubarb in the spring. Mine didn't thrive; it took me a few years to discover that it required more nourishment than many other things doing pretty well in the same soil. I began giving it manure and got splendid results. Now, since I have given up both chemical fertilizer and manure, it grows so abundantly with no food except vegetable garbage and dead leaves that I am constantly separating the roots and giving them away.

While we are on the subject, try this: cook up a pot of rhubarb with sugar to your taste and covered with water. Strain it through cheesecloth and serve the juice to people who think they don't like rhubarb. My experience is that they won't know what they are drinking but will almost certainly ask for a refill. Some of our friends like it so much that when it is out of season I keep a few containers in the freezer for them.

While we are speaking of mistakes, let's go back to my first one: that struggling little lilac hedge which I put in so eagerly and so ignorantly. I finally found out that a shrub needs a decent-sized hole and some good earth and undertook to dig up the hedge and do it properly. John saw me at it and said that while I was about it I might better put in some real bushes instead of twigs. He gave me some good-sized ones gathered from a big, old lilac bush he had.

However, I put back two of the "twigs" for comparison. Today, after twenty-five years, they are fair-sized bushes and I pick lilacs from them. The ones John gave me, though, are much larger and have many more blossoms.

As my ground and technique improved, I began getting enough tomatoes to drive me crazy, just as string beans, cucum-

bers and corn had long been doing. In the country it is sometimes a problem to find someone to give vegetables to at the
height of the season. If people don't grow them themselves, their
next-door neighbor probably does. When you think of all the
city people who would love to have them, it makes you feel sad.

One day I had a bushel of choice and truly beautiful tomatoes
on my hands and didn't know what on earth to do with them.
All of us, including the barn guests, were drinking quantities of
raw tomato juice, for you can get rid of more tomatoes if you
drink them instead of eating them.

When Dominick came that afternoon I asked him if he could
sell them. He said regretfully that all they were worth to him
was thirty cents.

I didn't sell them to him. I thought surely I could find someone to give them to, someone to whom they would be worth
more than thirty cents.

With a good deal of telephoning I finally located the neighbor of a friend who reluctantly consented to accept them if we
would deliver them. She would make some catsup with them,
although she had already made more than she wanted. Fred
took them to her and she warned him not to try to get her to
take any more.

However, that sort of thing happened rarely. I did find it a
big job to get rid of the surplus vegetables but, whether I gave
them away or sold them, they were appreciated and nothing was
wasted. That had a great deal to do with my unwillingness to
reduce the size of the garden.

Each year the soil improved a little, the crops were better, and
it seemed a big waste to abandon a source of pleasure to a good
many people. Almost everyone loves sun-ripened tomatoes and
corn fresh from the patch, and those two things took up the bulk
of the space in the garden.

I began selling the surplus vegetables to Dominick. The
prices I got were fantastically low, but I knew he was giving me
the wholesale market price. I often sold one hundred ears of as
fine corn as you could get anywhere for one dollar.

But even selling wholesale, to unseen customers, it seemed a pity to cut down. On his way to our place Dominick would take orders for corn (if I had told him I would have some for him that day) and would deliver it on his way home. Whenever I had to tell him I wouldn't have any for him the next time he came, his face would get long, sorry for his customers who would be so disappointed. Couldn't I spare just two dozen—one dozen? His people were spoiled now; they didn't want anything but my corn.

Generally speaking, I preferred selling vegetables to giving them away. You can give almost anything to almost anybody; few people are unkind enough or rude enough to refuse a gift. Selling is another matter; not very many people are kind enough or courteous enough to buy something they don't want. If someone buys your vegetables you can be relatively sure they will not put them into the garbage pail the minute your back is turned.

The farmers near by bought strawberries, asparagus, and late corn from me. They didn't grow strawberries because they were too much work, which was understandable. But the reason most of them gave for not growing asparagus baffled me: they would have to wait two years before they would have a full season's crop. From my limited observation I had concluded that farmers had both patience and foresight; their attitude to asparagus seemed to contradict that.

I never did get any satisfactory reason out of them as to why they almost never planted late corn. They seemed surprised and delighted when I had some to sell them after Labor Day.

One day I proudly told Bess and Henry Conescu, old friends and at the moment barn guests, that I had earned forty dollars the preceding summer by selling vegetables. Bess, a competent flower gardener and responsive to every phase of growing anything said that was splendid. But Henry scoffed.

"I'm impressed. You worked like a horse from dawn to dark, from April to October, and made forty bucks."

For a moment it did seem trivial, but only for a moment.

"You're all sorry for me because I'm foolish enough to work so hard," I answered him. "If I played tennis all summer everyone would say: 'Look what fun Ruth's having.' But tennis is more strenuous than gardening, and I don't like it half as much. I love to garden and I supply our table and the barn guests and I have forty dollars besides."

I said it with temporary fervor and conviction, but in my more honest moments I knew I wasn't being practical. In my ultra-honest moments I knew I often worked too hard and got too tired. Also, there was the memory of the look on my nephew Roger's face when he said something to me in praise of Mother's columbine, right there in the yard, and I replied: "Really? I must grab a minute and look at it."

It was undeniably a look of pity. I have often wondered why most people hate for their friends to be sorry for them. It seems to me that I would welcome a little pity if it was indicated.

But to be pitied when I thought I should be envied was quite another matter. And to have Roger sorry for me because I was behaving stupidly was beyond everything. Roger, of all people, who was supposed to think highly of me!

I lay awake that night (unheard of for me) thinking over the situation. I remembered that, as a little girl, I felt fate had played me a mean trick because I was born on Saturday.

> Born on Monday, fair of face,
> Born on Tuesday, full of grace,
> Born on Wednesday, fine and tall,
> Born on Thursday, best day of all,
> Born on Friday, loving and giving,
> Born on Saturday, *work for a living*,
> Born on Sunday, child that is blest
> With heavenly peace and rest.*

---

* I note that Bartlett's version of this is quite different, but this is the way we said it when we were children.

It went something like that, italics mine. As a child I saw no justice in my getting the worst day of the week.

Now, with an adult point of view, Monday and Wednesday seemed superficial; Tuesday, too, if it meant physical grace; Thursday—well, who wrote the verse? Who knows what the author called "best"?

Friday, loving—but not necessarily lovable; also giving— but with what motive? Skipping to Sunday—nobody could quarrel with heavenly peace and rest, and yet it sounded a bit too inactive. Saturday—no matter who wrote the verse, that day was explicit.

I worked for a living; the housework and cooking were a necessary contribution to our existence. It wouldn't be fair to count gardening; that was not an obligation. It was just my good fortune that the vegetables I grew were a welcome help to the budget.

I greatly preferred working for a living to merely working. I would have felt lonely and restless if I had been cut off from the majority of mankind—with almost everybody else working for a livelihood and me just keeping in motion for some artificial reason.

Not only that, I would have hated any other kind of setup. How perfectly awful if Fred had a lot of money and wanted to have a maid or two! How much more wearing to adjust to another personality than to scrub the kitchen floor and wash the windows! How humiliating to have to feel nervous and apologetic to the cook every time guests dropped in unexpectedly at mealtime!

Saturday's child was the lucky one.

Those were middle-of-the-night thoughts. In the morning I still approved of them, but added another: it was the unnecessarily large size of my project that made me ridiculous and a legitimate object of pity. If only I could preserve the surplus, all that work would be justified.

Canning was not a new thought. However, whenever someone had asked me before why I didn't do any preserving, I had replied with plenty of sarcasm: "Exactly which idle hour of the day do you suggest that I set aside for canning?"

But just now it didn't seem so impossible. We had recently replaced our oil cook stove with an electric one. Glancing through the small cookbook which had come with the new stove, I had seen that all one had to do to preserve vegetables was to put them raw into glass jars and set them in the oven for so and so long.

The morning after my sleepless night I got out the cookbook and reread these directions. It certainly didn't seem much of a trick. I picked everything, anyway; I could simply fill jars with my output instead of dashing about trying to find someone to give it to. I would try it. It even sounded restful, not to have to worry over what to do with what we couldn't use.

For once I chose to be moderate. Even if pressure canners had reached my consciousness I am not sure that I would have wanted one. I wasn't yet prepared to take a big step and begin to can everything. I was definitely going to be nonchalant about it; there were the tomatoes, there was an oven, there were even a lot of glass jars in the cellar that had been left there by the former owner. I didn't have to go out and buy a thing except some jar rubbbers. I didn't have to think of this as an activity of any size. Stick a few jars of tomatoes into the oven, once, and never do it again if I didn't feel like it. Ever since my tactics with the blueberries I had a high regard for my ability to circumvent any job that didn't appeal to me.

You're wrong—that first year I didn't preserve a single thing except tomatoes. I don't remember how many dozen quarts I put up. I filled all of the empty jars. However, by October I knew that I was headed for canning in a big way.

Actually, the tomatoes were so easy to do, even before I got a pressure canner, that I hardly noticed any inroads on my leisure that year. In spring and early summer I was still busy all day, but by August I could often spend an hour or two lying on the grass in the shade. I suppose I would have preferred the couch in our astonishingly cool living room, but no doubt I was showing off, letting everyone see that I had plenty of time to rest if I happened to want to.

The bees were showing off, too, but in a different way. In August by midafternoon they would have liked to knock off and call it a day, I was positive, but lazily, halfheartedly, they hovered over the flowers, pretending to work.

The ants were a nuisance. Instead of staying on the ground where they belonged, they roamed all over me, gaining no benefit from it, simply determined to shame me—they were busy fellows and had no time for napping. I had to brush them off carefully without killing them because Mary had convinced me that, by their purposeful energy and haste, you could tell they were hurrying to get through and go home and the family would be terribly upset if they didn't arrive there safely.

Fred gave me a look of infinite disgust when I asked him as casually as I could to drop into a store and buy six-dozen quart jars. I really wanted twelve-dozen quarts and four-dozen pints, but I thought it a little wiser to seem restrained.

This was in March; I had jars washed and ready for asparagus before the first stalk showed its tip above the ground. I was anxious about this new project; both the books and the neighbors made the canning of everything except tomatoes sound difficult and precarious. Besides, oven canning seemed to be something new and frowned on by some authorities.

I concentrate when I do even the simplest job, and interruptions throw me off badly. I had a chef's white cap which an impertinent friend had given me with the helpful suggestion that, if I wore it, I might learn to cook. I hunted it up and wore it for luck, but it also meant: Don't speak to me; I'm canning and I might make a fatal mistake.

The summer wasn't half over before I felt sure enough of myself to work without the cap. Canning is child's play when you get used to it.

I put up about two hundred jars of various vegetables that summer, not counting a hundred quarts of tomatoes, and there was no lying on the grass. I had not figured accurately; it took more time to can the vegetables than to find someone to give them to, or to sell them to Dominick.

For awhile I was amazed every time I opened a jar and found out that it hadn't spoiled, and I was almost childishly proud of that fine display in the cellar.

In the spring I astonished everybody, including myself, by having only half the garden plowed. I even deserted the lower half of that hand-dug asparagus. For I had discovered a fundamental fact which I must have known all along, but was trying to ignore: there were only twenty-four hours in each day and you had to use a few of them for sleeping.

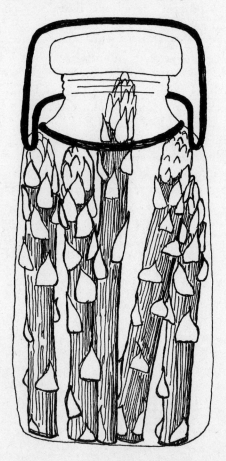

If You Have Tears

To START WITH, let's have a good cry over the muskmelons. Mary and I are both especially fond of a delicious melon. Our standard is high; in Kansas we became used to the best, and although that is a long time ago, we seem to remember how a melon ought to taste.

I grew them every year and produced beautiful ones, but the flavor was usually mediocre. I knew that something was definitely wrong, because a canteloupe which is allowed to stay on the vine until it comes off when you roll it gently is, other things being equal, far superior to a melon picked partly green, as those commercially grown have to be. And yet ours were no better than the commercial melons—sometimes not as good.

I knew that a sandy soil such as ours was supposed to be right for growing melons. When I began buying seeds from Joseph Harris and became convinced that I could trust them to tell the truth about quality, I bought what they recommended most highly for flavor. Also, I carefully followed their planting instructions.

About the fourth summer we had the most delicious melons we had eaten since the Kansas days. I had done nothing different that year and had no way of knowing why their flavor was superior. However, Mary and I were greatly encouraged and hoped that at last we would have excellent melons.

We didn't. Year after year we had a fine crop as far as quantity, size, beauty and aroma went, but the flavor was never so good again. The vines had always been green and healthy looking—no bugs, no disease.

One summer the yield was particularly heavy and the melons were large, fine looking, with firm, thick flesh, deep orange in color. They smelled like a refreshing perfume.

Because there were so many we kept count as we gathered them. There were 85, and as they ripened Mary and I took turns tasting them. One bite out of each—they were so flat and flavorless that we were disgusted and persuaded poor little Virginia to do the tasting. She knew a good melon, too, and she didn't have to say a word. The expression on her face was enough. We threw every one away.

I didn't give up, but I kept thinking and wondering about it. They had been of the highest quality in Kansas every season. What did Kansas have that Connecticut lacked? At last I pounced on it: hot weather, hot nights. Our nights are so cool that you always need one blanket, oftener two or three. Here in the valley we are several degrees colder than they are on the ridge, less than a mile away. Unfortunately, I couldn't remember whether or not we had had an unusually hot summer that year when our melons had been so delicious.

I wrote to Carl Warren and asked him if the cold nights could be our trouble; and he said, probably. So the next summer I tried raising three hills of melons in a movable cold frame, but the frame was too small for the spreading vines. Seven out of the eight melons I got were only fair; the eighth, which was excellent, ripened when Mary was in New York, and I had a hard time trying to enjoy it, since she is fonder of a good melon than I am.

So no more melons. John grows them; his place is higher than ours and never gets as cold. But it is pretty cold, too, and his melons aren't as good as a canteloupe is at its best. They are far better than those you buy, though, and of course he shares them with us.

I sometimes wonder if I would have wanted to live here in the valley if I had known about the short season, cold nights, frost even in June once in a long while. And one year we had frost on August 24th. Would I have wanted to live here if I had known that I couldn't grow melons, that the forsythia would bloom only three times in twenty-five years, that, some seasons, there would be no lilac blossoms? If I could have forseen all I would go through trying to raise strawberries, that it wasn't safe to plant annual flowers until June?

I don't know, but of course I am not sorry that we are here. If you like a challenge you could hardly choose a better place to live and have a garden. If it is the struggle that counts you are all set for life, for you will never stop struggling.

An occasional defeat is to be expected. However, fate could have been a little kinder, could have selected collards or Chinese cabbage rather than melons for conquering me, for putting me in my place.

I suppose it was inevitable that someday I would drop in my tracks, but it didn't seem fair and just that planting the seeds for those 85 worthless melons should be the cause of it. I had sacrificed some good novel-reading time the previous winter, checking up on my method of planting melons. I found out that I had been following the rules, but I elaborated on them, making the holes bigger, putting in more rotted manure than usual, mixing it more thoroughly than I had been doing.

With such complete information and the knowledge that my soil was exactly right for melons, naturally I put in a whole lot of hills. Wouldn't any optimist, if he loved melons?

There may be sensible people, however, who wouldn't have done it all in one day. I wasn't that sensible, and when I finished planting the last hill I had trouble getting to my feet. I hobbled to the house and got through until bedtime without telling anybody. I thought a night's rest would fix me up.

But I had a bad night and in the morning found that I couldn't get out of bed. My left thigh was killing me.

Fred called our good friend and doctor, Than Selleck, who said I had sciatica. Part of the treatment was rest in bed, no telling for how many days. He, together with the pain, cowed me completely. You could hardly imagine anyone as subdued as I was.

Nobody said, or even looked, "I told you so." They all thought, I'm sure, that I had had lesson enough and would spend my leisure time thinking of my stubbornness and resolving to reform.

What I did, actually, was to ask for my opera glasses and lie there on the bed on the upstairs screened porch overlooking the vegetable garden forty yards away and watch the weeds making hay while the cat was away.

I was brave and sweet-tempered and philosophical—really wonderful. I remarked cheerfully that I knew when I was licked. Fred and Hal guffawed. Hal said: "I always told you she was a smart gal. She knows the score. When she's flat on her back and can't move her leg she knows she can't go out and hoe corn all day."

This was in May; my pals, Virginia and Mary, weren't there. Fred hired a boy to do some cultivating and as soon as I could hobble with a cane (about a week or ten days, I think it was) I went to see how he was making out. He was far from what you could call an experienced gardener; I was terribly tempted to give him some advice and teach him a thing or two, but I had a definite feeling that he wouldn't profit by it. Obviously hoeing was just a boring job to him, poor boy; I gave him an insincere compliment and limped back to the house.

I think the experience taught me a little something. I don't believe I worked quite so incessantly after that. Oh, yes, it did teach me one valuable trick. I learned to vary my posture: kneel awhile, hoe awhile, bend, squat, hoe, kneel.

This procedure stood me in good stead when I had my terrific battle with witch grass. If you are a beginner you may not know what that is. It is a great deal harder to cope with than the crab grass which gets in your lawn and annoys you. It behaves like asparagus; that is, you can't kill it by piling leaves or hay on it as you can ordinary grass, weeds, or other plants. Like asparagus, it creeps under the ground and reaches up right through anything you put on top of it. Even if you put a

wide board on a spear of witch grass. it will defeat you by
creeping under the board until it gets to the edge of it, then it
comes up again. Not defiantly—nonchalantly, which makes you
even madder.

One morning in late May I went to the garden and started
to cultivate the young parsley. I came across some grass which
baffled me because there seemed to be no end to the root. It
ran along under the ground like a piece of thick white string
and pretty soon another green shoot showed up, and another,
and another. I was puzzled; I had never seen nor heard of
witch grass.

I realized that it was no ordinary problem because the white
part ran along under the parsley and it was difficult to get it
out without injuring the tiny plants. I worked away at it,
slowly and painstakingly, not even wondering if it was very
widely spread. It didn't occur to me that it could be, overnight.
I hadn't noticed it the day before.

Arthur Burr came in around noon delivering milk. He and
I were always exchanging joys, troubles, vegetables, and flowers,
and now I told him about this strange grass I had found. When
I described it he said with real concern: "Sounds to me like
witch grass. Is there much of it?"

"No, I don't think so. I only saw a little around the parsley,"
I said.

"Let's have a look."

We went to the garden. I was a little fearful because Art has
an expressive face and he looked seriously disturbed. He wandered around the garden, his face getting long as, over and
over, he bent down and pulled out a spear of witch grass.

"It's all over the place, every foot of it," he said finally,
reluctantly, his voice and face sober with sympathy.

"What can I do, Art?"

"I don't know. I'll ask my father, see if he has any suggestions."

The next day Art reported that witch grass was the number-one enemy of the farmer in the way of weeds, that you couldn't even plow and turn it under, for it only kept on thriving.

"What does a person do, then, when it's all through the garden?" I asked.

Art is one of the kindest people I know. I could see how he hated to answer that.

"My father says that when a man gets it in his garden as bad as you've got it he gives up that spot and plows up another place that's free of it. I'll do it for you right away if you want me to."

This was my tenth year of gardening. Art knew there was quite a lot of manure there because, since Charlie's cow had died, he had put it there. He knew all about the sand and stones which the road men had contributed, knew what I had gone through to rehabilitate that spot after it had been almost ruined. He was as sorry for me as I was for myself.

"Can't I spade it out?" I asked hopefully.

"How big is it now, 120 by 100? Take a lifetime because you can't just spade, you'd have to stop with every spadeful and shake out and get rid of every root."

I told him I'd think it over and he left me with my sorrow.

I thought of John; he was as kind as Art and a good friend and sometimes Fred hired him to do some jobs around the place. I would ask him if he would help me with it. In the meantime I began carefully getting the witch grass out from under my precious strawberry plants.

John couldn't have been more sympathetic, but he said the same thing Art had said: it would take forever. He couldn't possibly spare the time and, anyway, it would cost too much.

"You'd have to be a fool or have the patience of a Chinaman to do a job like that," he said.

That gave me an idea: there was a Chinese who lived a mile or so away; he was very friendly and he loved the earth and I might persuade him to do it. I asked him but he, too, said that it would take forever, he was too busy, and it would cost too much.

I thought of John's remark: only a fool or a Chinaman would attempt it. I wasn't a Chinaman, but I had done so many foolish things in my life that I had no good reason to believe that I wasn't a fool. I would do it myself.

I did. Art and John and my other farmer friends were aghast when they saw what I was attempting to do. Fred and John said I was completely nuts; I knew the others thought so too, but they weren't rude enough to say it. But when, come fall, there was not a spear of witch grass left in the garden and I had had my usual crops and was still alive, they all willingly admitted that I had done the wise thing.

One problem remained. Wherever witch grass bordered on the garden (which luckily was on only one side of it) I was faced with the job for the rest of my life of constantly pulling it out to keep it from invading the garden again. After long and arduous thinking I decided to dig a ditch all along that side of the garden, narrow, but deep enough to go below the roots of the witch grass. Fortunately the grass was along the asparagus side of the garden where the ditch wouldn't interfere with plow or wheelbarrow.

Witch grass can creep, but it can't jump a trench. If it has emotions it probably sits there on the wrong side of the ditch wishing passionately that it could get to the other side. Praying, if witch grass prays, that some fine spring I'll forget to check up to see that the ditch is still deep enough to outwit it. I won't forget.

Through that whole summer it was just my hard luck that those friends and friends of friends vacationing in the barn weren't the kind who would have enjoyed helping me with my big project. I am serious about not wanting people to work in the garden unless they enjoy it. Also, it's an advantage if they know what they're doing and pull up weeds instead of vegetables.

Virginia was now twenty years old, engaged to Millard, and came out only with him, for week ends. Mary was busy in New York. So I had no help with the witch grass.

One day a girl who knew nothing at all about gardening

asked me to give her something to do. I put her to work on a flower bed, showing her how to proceed. Presently Fred came to me and asked me what I had told her to do.

"Thin the petunias," I said.

He laughed.

"She told me she was weeding the potatoes. Even I knew that couldn't be right, there in the lawn."

Fred loved to tell tall stories to the ignorant New Yorkers. He told one girl that the way to grow succotash was to cut open a lima bean, put a grain of corn inside, and plant it. He still swears that she believed him.

Broadly speaking, the barn guests who insisted on helping were a hindrance. Almost all of them had to be supervised every minute. Bess Conescu and Ed Carlson were exceptions; they knew how to garden and were a big help. On some jobs, though, Ed's artistic feeling stood in the way of efficiency; he couldn't take the beauty of the strawberries in his stride and too often not only he, but I also, had to stop work to admire them.

Henry Conescu knew nothing about gardening, but he could watch Bess and me planting something for about ten minutes, never asking a question, and then pitch in and do it exactly right. Quicker and better than we did.

The barn always had someone in it. On week ends it overflowed and I tried to stay out of the garden on Saturday afternoons and Sundays. For one thing I believed in taking a rest; for another, keeping people out of the garden was impossible if I was out there. They were more persistent than the gnats.

At best, they distracted me by talking to me, tramped on the plants, and even if they stayed in the path packed it down so hard that it meant extra work when I had to cultivate. At worst, they insisted on helping.

I hesitated to tell people that they were standing on the young plants. They were so stricken when I did that they usually got excited and began prancing about trying to find the proper place to stand, and by the time I got them safely into a path, more damage had been done that if I had let them alone.

Before we leave this tearful chapter let us record two additional griefs. The big lilac bush at the corner of the house didn't bloom at all the first three years. I pruned it and put wheel-barrowsful of manure around it to no avail. Through the twenty-five years it has had a few stray blossoms which seem to be saying: "Oh, well, for pity's sake, stop whimpering. Smell us— one thousand more would smell stronger, but no sweeter. What do you need so many for, anyway? You can't take them with you."

As for Old Baldy, along with most of the other thirty-one apple trees he finally died a natural death. We never pruned nor sprayed the apple trees; it is much too expensive unless you are going to sell the apples, and who would pick them? Not Fred, and as for me, I don't believe in climbing ladders after your bones begin to get brittle. I am very good at falling down our steep, 200-year-old stairs without hurting myself, and frequently do. But I see no point in challenging your luck, and I am not going to fall off a ladder, ever. The only way I know of to make absolutely sure of that is not to get on one.

Fourteen years had gone by. I had produced and canned a lot of vegetables, but I had worked too hard. I had not been living up to my faith, for I profoundly believed that my first obligation to the people around me was to do my very best to create a pleasant, relaxed, happy atmosphere. I could not do that when I was overtired, but I didn't have to work until I reached that point.

The garden had been only partly successful. Melons were a complete failure. Peppers were temperamental, blowing hot and cold. Lima beans could be relied on never to mature. Lettuce, beets, and spinach all behaved halfheartedly. Their indifference to achievement seemed colossal.

My enthusiasm never wavered. I still loved to help people start a garden, and I'm afraid I talked about growing things a little more than was desirable. As Fred put it: "Ruth may not have a green thumb, but she has a green tongue."

Now we enter a new era—an end to old-fashioned garden-ing, the beginning of leisure and, God remaining neutral, sure and splendid crops.

Throw Away Your Spade and Hoe

Now AND THEN there is a morning so beautiful it makes you feel
that all the world, and heaven too, has had a conference and
voted to create one perfect thing. When you have rejoiced in
the splendor all around you, you close your eyes, the better to
drink in the sounds. There are not only birds, singing and calling
from the trees—there is also music in the grass. You are afraid
to take one step for fear you will tread upon some lovely and
mysterious sound.

On one of these brilliant mornings I wandered aimlessly out
to the vegetable garden, aimlessly because it was not yet plowed
and there was nothing for me to do there until it was.

One maddening thing about gardening is the plowing or
spading, whichever one you do. If you hire someone to plow
and harrow, it is not possible to have it done piecemeal. This
means that the whole plot should be plowed early in April in
order to get the peas, spinach, lettuce and parsley started on
time. But if you do that, the part where you will put your late
crops is lying idle through April, May and part of June. No,
not idle, that's the trouble; it is growing a fine crop of weeds
if there is rainy weather. And if it is dry the sun is baking the
soil. I have heard many a busy farmer complain that he had
to plow again in May because the ground had become so hard
he couldn't plant.

If you spade your garden, of course you can dig up just
as much as you are ready to use. However, that means that the
rest of it is producing weeds, some of them perennial and mean
to handle.

I never once got all the early things in on time during those first fourteen years. I got peas planted by digging a trench for them, and could have done the same for spinach and lettuce if I had wanted to use my time and strength that way, but I didn't want to. So I got them in too late and the spinach always gave up before it reached its full growth. As for the lettuce, it was so poor that at least there was one advantage: it tempted no invaders since it wasn't even fit for a rabbit, let alone a king. One can, of course, buy lettuce plants and I did one season, but I don't like transplanting and the lettuce wasn't successful enough to tempt me to do it again.

Arthur Burr had been plowing and harrowing the garden of late years and I knew he did it only because he hated to refuse me. He was far too busy to want to bother with it and so, once I had hesitantly mentioned it at the end of March, there was no use to try to hurry him. I knew he would do it just as soon as he could.

Then at the critical moment the tractor always breaks down, and April of 1944 was no exception to this rule. Art was ready to plow, but the tractor wouldn't go.

So now on this perfect morning I stood there in the garden, longing to put in some seeds. I wandered over to the asparagus bed and said to it affectionately: "Bless your heart, you don't have to wait for anyone to plow you. You merely—"

I stopped short as a thought struck me like a blow. One never plows asparagus and it gets along fine. Except for new sod, why plow anything, ever?

Why plow? Why turn the soil upside down? *Why* plow?

I AM NOT GOING TO. I AM GOING TO PLANT!

I don't suppose I actually shouted the words aloud, but they were making a deafening uproar in my head and even in my heart. The things in me which had, at one time and another, been subjects of comment for those who bothered to notice— my extremism, radicalism of various kinds, ignorance of and indifference to convention, to the status quo, to the written word, to the "established" fact—all of these unfashionable qualities rushed in now and took over. I would ask no one's advice or opinion, I would tell no one until I had done it, but just as sure as God made rebels and nonconformists I was going to ignore custom and tradition and I was going to plant right now.

It was my good fortune that, in spite of all warnings against it, I had formed the habit of leaving all the vegetable waste, such as corn stalks, right there in the garden and had spread leaves all over it in the fall and vegetable garbage all winter long. Now, when I raked this mass of stuff aside to make a row for the spinach I found the ground so soft and moist that I made a tiny drill with my finger. I had expected to be obliged to get out the little single-wheeled contraption I used for making a deep furrow, but with such soft earth it wasn't necessary.

I didn't have a qualm; I was terribly elated. I thought that Columbus must have felt almost as excited as this when he discovered America.

If it really worked, in May and June the ground would surely be soft enough to put in corn, beans and the other late things. With all these leaves no weeds would come through. Some did, however. The mulch wasn't thick enough.

Art and John thought I was off my head. The other farmers and neighbors shrugged shoulders, laughed, or seemed politely interested, according to their various temperaments.

Bursting with pride months, or perhaps years, before I had any right to be, I was more than a little let down when someone gave me a copy of *Plowman's Folly* by William Faulkner. He had stolen my idea of not plowing even before I had thought of it.

I found that Mr. Faulkner recommended sowing a green crop and harrowing it in. That would have been no answer to my problem. Art couldn't get around to harrowing any sooner than he could to plowing.

I found nothing in *Plowman's Folly* about using over-all mulch the year round to keep out weeds. As for the green crop he recommended for replenishing the soil, leaves and other vegetation would rot and replenish the earth. Then put on more.

Even that first year I began to visualize the utopia I had thought up for everyone who wanted to grow his own vegetables. Besides the expense, in our community (and I should think in many others) it is not easy to find someone to plow and harrow for you and often impossible to get it done just when you want it. The alternative, spading, is quite a job. Eliminate these things and eliminate also hoeing, weeding, cultivating—it sounded like science fiction and yet I believed in it. I didn't guess then the scope of it: no chemical fertilizer, no poison spray, no expensive manure, no laboriously built compost pile.

Most people wrinkle their noses and look disgusted when I suggest that they put their garbage on the garden.

"It is so much trouble to bury it," is the first objection.

"Don't bury it," I tell them. "Just toss it back where it came from. If you mulch, stick it under some hay. If you have cleanly cultivated rows tuck it around things like cabbage, cauliflower, rhubarb, where it won't show. It doesn't have to look ugly."

"It's not only the looks, it's the smell," almost everyone complains. "How could I stand such a stench in my garden?"

These people need to be educated. Let's have a look at what Mr. Webster has to say: "Garbage:—refuse animal or vegetable matter from a kitchen, market, or store;—anything worthless or filthy; refuse." And "refuse" Mr. Webster defines as "worthless matter."

The garbage I use in the garden has no animal matter of any kind, because that would no doubt attract dogs, cats, and other animals, which would be undesirable. It is no trick at all to keep meat scraps and bones separated from the rest of the garbage which is composed almost entirely of the waste part of vegetables and fruits and the left overs on the dinner plates. What is repellent about these things? They were quite inoffensive before you tossed them into the garbage pail. Why do they change character the minute they lose their individuality and become garbage?

The fact that we choose to call them garbage, refuse, worthless matter doesn't make them repulsive. No less an authority than Shakespeare has told us there is nothing in a name. There has to be some other reason, and if you will excuse me for saying so it is your own fault if your garbage is smelly. You dump waste matter into a garbage pail and let it stay there, pressed together and with no air, until it begins to smell badly.

I dislike bad smells intensely and I hate to clean a garbage pail. That is why I threw out the garbage pail long before I began to think of garbage as something valuable instead of as something worthless. I use a small pan, sitting conveniently on the sink, so small that no matter how lazy I feel I am obliged to empty it before it has a chance to become obnoxious. On a rainy day I sometimes tuck the refuse under the peonies, just outside the kitchen door. It doesn't show at all and please don't make a face; surely you have put manure on your roses and peonies, not to mention your strawberries.

So what is this vile stuff I ask you to throw on your garden? Outside leaves of cabbage, potato, turnip and beet peelings, pea hulls, corn husks—things which, if you had never brought them in from the garden, would not have to be embarrassed by their bad odor. And food left on plates, which is so far from being disgusting until your treatment of it makes it so that it would have been in your mouth instead of the garbage pail if your appetite had held out a few minutes longer.

When you throw all these things into the garden they are simply returning home, where they belong. The exceptions are egg shells and orange and grapefruit peels. These look out of place; I always hide them under the rhubarb or a bit of hay.

My rhubarb has been fed nothing but kitchen garbage— refuse—"worthless matter" for many years. One look at it and anybody will call Mr. Webster a liar, for the "filthy" stuff has been worth its weight in manure to the rhubarb.

I am sorry to go into such length on so humble a subject, but I have found that it takes quite a speech to convince my fellow gardeners that garbage is not, in itself, a filthy thing.

It is the bad habit of hanging onto it until it smells that makes it filthy.

As the weeds began to come through the inadequate mulch I frantically looked around for anything I could find which I could throw on the garden. Fred got out the scythe and cut some grass and weeds for me and I went through the meadow with a sickle and gathered everything I could. It was as much work as hoeing and weeding and not half as enjoyable. But I was beginning to see a glorious future opening out ahead of me, something to work toward, something to accomplish, something to prove.

All through my life I had every now and then invented— no, that isn't the right word—pulled out of the air, rather, a new and sometimes startling idea which I was sure would be of benefit to mankind. The pattern which ran through them was simplification of living, and perhaps that was why none of them took. People don't want to live simply, they want to compete, not only in business, but in furnishing their homes, buying their cars and clothes and even their food. If things get so complicated that you are worried and upset, don't take a little thought to try to rearrange and simplify your life—grab another cocktail and forget it for the moment.

Am I preaching? I'm sorry, but I feel badly when I see people clawing at the bars of a cage whose door is standing open.

I was having trouble putting this new idea of mine across, too, even with my most openminded and intelligent friends. This was a war year and Marcelle Krutch and I were doing some bartering; she gave me eggs and chickens and I gave her fresh and canned vegetables. She came over one day to bring some eggs and I could hardly wait to show her my project.

"But where's the garden?" she asked, puzzled.

"There. You're looking at it."

"What? That rubbish heap!" she cried.

It was early in the season; things weren't up yet and that,

I am afraid, was what it looked like the first year and only a little less so the second and third years.

Art became interested in it; John was thoroughly disgusted with me and it. Fred and Mary reserved judgment. Because of the rationing of gas Rex and Scott didn't get to see it.

Dad had died in the thirties and Mother in 1940. She went, thank God, too early to see the war (particularly hard to take for a good Quaker), but also too soon to enjoy my great discovery. I often think how interested she would be in it if she was living.

Virginia's face when she first saw it was a study. She was married now, but a part of her never left Poverty Hollow. She had always gone right along with me, full of enthusiasm; now she turned troubled eyes to mine and said: "Ruth, it looks so awful! Why don't you retreat? If the old way is too much work for you I'll ask Millard for a divorce and come and help."

The first three years were a struggle and a mess and I often longed for her. But I must reassure all prospective mulchers: those first years needn't have been difficult. Once you get it into your head that you have to put on *enough* mulch, six or eight inches deep, you do it, relax and enjoy your leisure.

It took me a long time to realize how much was necessary. It was hard to find enough; then I remembered that I had heard farmers talk about spoiled hay and I asked Art if he had any. He did and said if I could get someone to bring it down to me I was welcome to it. I got a great load of it, and that autumn I covered the whole garden thickly with leaves and hay to lie there over the winter.

"Spoiled hay" can be defined simply as any hay that is not fit to feed to the livestock. It may be mouldy; for mulch that doesn't matter.

Any hay, however "spoiled," is fine for mulch. Some kinds rot more quickly than others. The advantage is that your soil becomes enriched more rapidly; the disadvantage, you must put on a fresh supply a little sooner.

Salt hay is relatively expensive; it is pleasant to handle, clean and goodlooking. It rots extremely slowly and is an excellent mulch if you can afford it and if your soil is so rich that you are in no hurry to replenish it. The fact that salt hay is completely free of weed seeds is of no advantage in a well-mulched garden, for there weed seeds never get a break. I wouldn't be afraid to broadcast dandelion seeds all over my garden. The poor little things would die of old age before they had a chance to reproduce their kind.

That same autumn I switched from rotted to fresh manure. Everyone seems to be terrified of fresh manure, but if you are reasonably careful you won't injure a thing and it has more value than that which has rotted.

I began spreading fresh manure on the asparagus and Art's spoiled hay on top of it. I was through with one big job forever. If you feed your asparagus bed as much as it requires you also grow a healthy and prolific crop of weeds. Now I had stopped those before they started. Not only that, it was but a few years later when my soil became so rich that I abandoned manure entirely and then there were only two things to do in order to have asparagus, neither one of them arduous: spread hay on it and pick it.

For the other vegetables I had to rake away the mulch in order to plant. Then I would mark the row with a very little lime (more for lettuce, beets and spinach) make a tiny furrow and drop the seeds. I then covered the row with strips of cardboard and pulled the mulch back up to it. I find this an excellent system. Things seem to sprout more quickly (although I haven't checked that) and the ground stays soft and moist. I don't need much cardboard, since seeds are planted at different times. Of course I have to watch carefully not to leave the boards on after the little shoots break through the earth.

By the fourth season I was really launched and on my way. The soil was becoming so rich and black that I gave up all chemical fertilizers. I had always hated to handle the smelly stuff and that was a most pleasant parting of the ways.

Now the mulch was adequate; if I got lonesome for a weed

I had to go and visit some timid friend who had not yet been converted. I had not got around yet to trying to make the garden look attractive and that was what made most people hesitate to follow my example. But it looked better than it had at first; it was no longer the rubbish heap Marcelle had justifiably called it.

Year after year the ground became richer and more fluffy and I stopped buying manure. John had gone away for an indefinite stay; I did so long to make him eat his unkind words about my project! Everything became so luxuriant that, by the fourth season, I used only half of the space and mulched the other half, expecting to rotate each year. It was now so rich I couldn't bear to give it up entirely and, covered with mulch, I didn't have to work all of it.

Several years before she died Mother had had Charlie Stauffer build her a cottage on a huge rock to the left of our house. She and Mary had lived there nine months of the year. Now Mary was renting it, and when Bethany and Cal Kallgren moved in Bethany wanted to grow vegetables. I was glad to let her have the half of the garden I wasn't using.

She had never put a seed of anything into the ground in her life and I would have to teach her, which would be a pleasure. But I hardly knew her when I offered to let her work right there by my side. I was a little apprehensive; she seemed shy and retiring, but the quietest girl can turn out to be a chatterbox when she comes to know you well enough to feel easy with you.

On occasion I have said (and I think perhaps I mean it seriously) if I could choose one fault which my husband must not have, it would be the habit of talking too much. I can hardly stand a chain talker, no commas, no periods, no new paragraphs. It is bad enough when I am doing nothing and can concentrate on not listening to him, but when I am trying to do something, talking (either my own or somebody else's) confuses and exhausts me.

We have a big hospitable kitchen which smilingly tempts all

the dinner guests to gather there with their cocktails and enter-
tain the cook-hostess. Sometimes, in desperation, I tell them
about the cook my grandmother once had who, when people
got too thick around her, would say: "I guess I'd better go to
bed and get out of the way."

This story never helped much. Even those who got the
hidden meaning behind the story proper thought it applied to
everybody but them.

Fred isn't one to help in the kitchen, but of late years he
does something far better. He invites everyone out of the kitchen
and sees to it that they accept the invitation.

To have people talk to me when I am in the garden is the
same thing, only more so. I would like my kitchen to be my
castle, but I want more than that from my garden. It is my
cathedral, my sanctuary. No, I don't mean cathedral, I mean
Friends' Meeting House, where the keynote is quietness.

I could have said all that more briefly and less fancifully:
as most of us do I need a certain amount of privacy and I
prefer not to be obliged to lock myself in the bathroom in
order to get it.

Bethany never once got in my hair. After she had been
gardening with me for a week or so Cal came in and said how
much she was enjoying it.

I said: "I like teaching her. She attends to her business and
there's never a peep out of her."

Cal laughed, and when I looked at him with a question in
my eyes he told me: "That's exactly what she says about you."

And Fred remarked: "When two introverts get together
everybody's happy."

Bethany and Cal lived in the cottage until they outgrew it
by adding to their family. Bethany had a successful garden
(mulched, of course) for three summers.

Then Jim and Shelby Baker moved in and Shelby tried a
garden for one year. She was as satisfactory to work alongside
of as Bethany, but she gave it up after the first summer.

Now nobody had use for that spot which I had lovingly

cared for through twenty-two years. It had become a rich and valuable little piece of ground. But I didn't need it, so once again I cut my garden in half, to fifty by sixty feet.

It was silly, I decided, to have a garden bigger than one needed. Heaven forbid that I should do anything silly!

My Garden Is My Compost Pile

I DON'T LIKE TO MAKE FUN OF ANYBODY, even including my betters, but I do have to smile sometimes at the mental convolutions the experts are going through in regard to compost piles. Do this, don't do that, put on this, not too little, but be careful, not too much; wet it, but not too wet; now—no, we've changed our minds, this is better. *Now* we've got it—no, wait a minute—

Don't misunderstand me; I am not against experimentation and attempts toward improvement in any field. I am sure that compost piles give you some mighty fine dirt. In the meantime, however, while the experts wrinkle their foreheads and write articles and the gardeners carry and pile and dampen and turn their material I am enjoying splendid compost all the time over my entire garden.

I didn't go through a lot of hard work, either, to put it there. I didn't pile up this and heap on that, put on this to make it rot, wet it for this reason, but not too wet for that reason, turn it over every so often and wait then for it to become good dirt. And when it did, I didn't have to go through the tedious hard work of carting it from where it was to where I wanted it. It was already there.

The dirt made by building a compost pile is a very desirable thing to have, but the man who goes through all the antics necessary to make this pile is to be pitied unless he has a great deal of time and energy he wouldn't know what to do with otherwise. He is like a man, let us say, who is suffering from a physical ailment and knows of a plant, growing on a far mountain, which will cure him. He makes the long, hard journey, finds the plant and is cured.

He is well satisfied until he returns home and finds that this plant also grows in his back yard. He had no way of knowing that until he saw the plant on the mountain and compared the two.

And so it is with those who build compost piles; they don't know any better way to make rich dirt. Now you are hearing of an easier, better way; you need no longer climb a mountain for your compost. It is yours for a small fraction of that labor.

My way is unscientific, but it has produced fine vegetables for eleven years. I simply spread mulch where I want the compost to be eventually. It rots and becomes rich dirt, with the valuable by-products of keeping down weeds, keeping the earth soft, holding moisture and eliminating plowing and spading, hoeing and cultivating.

I use lime, of course, to keep the soil from getting too acid and I put some cotton-seed meal on the strawberries, lettuce, spinach, corn and beets. This supplies the nitrogen they might otherwise lack.

The lettuce I grow now is crisp, fine flavored, solid and as big as your head with a sombrero on it. All the other crops are praiseworthy, not to say sensational: pepper plants with fifteen or more large peppers on each; huge heads of cauliflower; a ten-foot row of kohlrabi producing eighty perfect specimens; tender, crisp carrots, big enough sometimes for one to make a meal for five people. Everything else to match.

I have gardened like this for eleven years and I am satisfied with it. However, for those people who are so constituted that they must know by analysis rather than by results that they have an adequate soil for growing things, nothing could be easier than to have their soil analyzed and to add anything they may find lacking. They can still take advantage of this easy, effective way of building compost.

It is unfortunate that the use of chemical fertilizer is not only a practical and scientific question, but also a commercial one.

After I had done over-all mulching for several years I gave a talk on the radio about it, but I was not permitted to say that I used no chemical fertilizer. I told them that I wouldn't say one shouldn't use it, simply that I didn't, but even that was not allowed.

Of course, I wouldn't expect any magazine that advertises chemical fertilizer and poison sprays to take kindly to my way of gardening. These periodicals are obviously nervous over the strides which organic gardening has made. I haven't noticed how it is lately, but for a long while I hardly ever picked up a garden magazine without seeing at least one article which was trying to frighten people into using chemical fertilizer. You were simply done for if you didn't. They were all but hysterical about it. These articles were often featured on the covers and must have given organic gardeners considerable satisfaction. It wasn't necessary formerly to try to persuade people to use these fertilizers; they used to take it for granted that that was the thing to do.

Who can blame these magazines for putting up a battle for chemical fertilizers and poison sprays? Advertising these things is a large part of their income. Who among us sacrifices his bread and butter or even his Cadillac for the general good? It is so human to make a mistake or even cheat a little about something which threatens our feeling of security. We could be in a chronic stew about this lack of integrity, but who wants ulcers?

I respect scientists and experts up to a point; I am even willing to help them out if only they would let me. After ten years of over-all mulching and the making of compost in my easy way I read a short, signed article in *Science News Letter* which warned against trying to garden without the use of chemical fertilizer. I wrote to them and told them of my experience. Not only did nobody rush to Poverty Hollow to have a look, my letter wasn't acknowledged.

I wrote to *Consumers' Union* twice about my experience. The second time I sent them an article I had written about

mulch, published in *Organic Gardening and Farming*. I wanted
to show them that I had had some slight recognition in the field.
I chose these two publications to write to because neither of
them advertised fertilizer and I thought they would be openminded.

I got nowhere. Gardeners from different parts of the country
had written me excited letters asking further questions about
over-all mulching; my article had been reprinted in Melbourne,
Australia. But *Consumers' Union*, whose mission, I had always
thought, was to serve the public, remained uninterested. I was
disappointed. They have articles on gardening, they talk about
spading and making compost piles, never bothering to find out
if that work is really necessary. Certainly I didn't expect them
to believe me, but I had foolishly hoped they would look into it.
They had the means to spread the good news, if they decided
it was good news; I hadn't, with all garden magazines automatically opposed to my message. It has occurred to me recently that
perhaps I should have pointed out to *Consumers' Union* that
mulching is not synonymous with organic gardening. One can,
of course, use over-all mulching and also add chemical fertilizer
if one wants to. I can't think of any reason for wanting to.

When I first heard of organic gardening (I was then already
mulching) and read about its claims that this method eliminated
pests, I muttered: "Tut, tut! That is going a little far." And then
forgot about it.

I had always hated the job of spraying poison on plants, but
I had done it through the years pretty conscientiously. About
the time I began to mulch I said to Art that I loathed fooling
with poison sprays and he told me that someone he knew had
controlled all pests effectively by keeping his plants covered
with lime.

I tried that for awhile with fair success. Then, the third
summer after I had started to mulch everything, it rained so
frequently and washed off the lime so often that I gave up and
didn't do anything about the bugs. And yet I saw almost none.

The following season I used neither lime nor poison. The

tomatoes were clean; there was not one corn borer; only a handful of Mexican beetles instead of the thousands I had always had to contend with. The next year I boldly discarded the habit of putting little paper collars around the pepper and tomato plants. Not one was cut off by a cut worm. And I didn't see one bean beetle that second year.

Freedom from pests! For me that alone would have been enough to tie me to mulching for life, without all of the bigger advantages.

Why did all the unwelcome little creatures snoot my fine produce now? Of course I don't know the answer to that. When I told Rex about it he said: "We'll just have to call it a miracle until we find out the reason."

John came back after having been away two years. When he saw my rich soil he could hardly believe my story. He kept trying to get me to admit that someone had given me dozens and dozens of loads of manure.

"Is that really the gravel you used to try to grow stuff in?" he asked incredulously.

John began to mulch with as good results as I was having. I was glad that he had a heavy soil, for this question had been raised: Over-all mulching is perfect for your light, sandy soil, but would it be as good for my heavy one? John settled that question in the affirmative.

Here is something interesting: the books will tell you that onions will not grow in all soils. They don't tell you what to do about it; they simply say they won't grow. This had been true about John's soil. For twenty years he had tried to grow onions and had finally given up. He couldn't even get decent scallions from sets. For some years he had had a little spot in my garden where he grew his onions.

After he had mulched for three years I said to him in the spring: "Let's go out and choose a spot for your onions."

"Not this year," he said. "My soil is beginning to look like yours now. I'm going to plant my onions up home."

I couldn't persuade him to try some in each place. He planted seeds and Sweet Spanish plants in his own garden and had onions that weighed just under one and one-half pounds apiece.

I have, of course, told every gardener I know about mulching and a great many of them are doing it now. It appeals to the man who works all day and wants a garden, and who now can have one without the weeds constantly getting ahead of him. It appeals to mothers with young children who are glad they do not have to give up the vegetables they need and the flowers they love. It appeals to those who are getting old and are facing the unpleasant thought of being obliged to stop growing things. It appeals to people like my nephew Roger and his wife, Gerry, who would rather read a book or have a swim than work in the garden, but who want their yard to be attractive. I spent a few week ends giving them a start; now they can read, swim, pick tulips, peonies, roses, chrysanthemums, and even tomatoes, with never a weed to reproach them.

The local Ladies' Guild asked me to talk to them about my method. I am not a speech maker and wondered how I would make out. My subject saw me through. The women could not wait for me to finish before they began waving their hands, eager to ask questions.

In the preceding chapter I said that when I first thought of this way of planting I decided that nothing but sod ever needed to be plowed. I now realize that even sod need not be turned over.

Bethany and Cal Kallgren have their own home now, and when they chose a spot covered with grass for their garden they intended to have it plowed. Since the top soil had been removed from this plot, they expected to have to plow it and then cover it again with top soil.

When Bethany took me over to look at it I advised them to skip the plowing, put on the top soil and then a thick covering of leaves and hay. They have done that. Since they imported their top soil they can have a garden this coming spring. Otherwise, they would have had to wait longer until the mulch had rotted the sod. I have no idea how long that would take, probably too long to be practical. Somebody should try it.

Some people hesitate to adopt over-all mulching because they prefer the looks of a neatly cultivated garden. I used to, but now a garden with the earth exposed to the burning, baking sun looks helpless and pathetic to me. It looks fine if someone has just cultivated it after a good rain, but how often is that the case? At all other times an unmulched garden looks to me like some naked thing which, for one reason or another, would be better off with a few clothes on.

Piecemeal mulching is nothing new. People have mulched strawberries for many years to keep them clean. Why are mulched peas and carrots uglier than mulched strawberries?

A flourishing garden with clean hay spread neatly between the rows looks attractive to me, and comfortable.

I read somewhere recently the theory that corn and tomatoes should not be mulched because they need the heat of the sun around the roots. This has not been proven and I have another theory to present. Possibly these things need, rather, an even temperature which they do not get with a hot sun in the daytime and cool nights. With a mulch the temperature is much more nearly even than without it.

I can add this: only through these years since my corn has been mulched do I almost always get two fine ears from each stalk, and I now plant it more closely than the books advise. If the tomatoes suffer from being mulched they are very brave about it and keep it to themselves. I have never seen any indication that they mind at all.

I believe that growing old (and I don't mean from fifty to seventy, I mean from seventy to ninety) can well be the most delightful and exhilarating part of a person's life. I realize that those are almost fighting words and I am acquainted with many of the arguments against them. But my belief in them is a strong one and has a bearing on my present method of gardening.

Roughly, it seems to me that there are two ways of getting

old. One is to expect and accept it; that is, expect to become more and more incapacitated, to hear and see less well, to remember less well, sleep less, eat less, care less. These people, perhaps, give in too soon; life becomes a thing to bear, not to enjoy.

The other way of getting old is to fight old age. These people won't give an inch until they must. And when they must, they resent having to. You all know these old people; they don't grow old happily.

I will soon be seventy-one years old and I have thought out a way to avoid falling into the second pitfall, which is the one into which my temperament would have plunged me. I used a trick which I thought up as a child: if I foresaw that someone was going to make me do something I didn't want to do, I hurried up and did it before I was told to, thus hardly minding it at all. Probably enjoying my cunning.

One day last summer I faced the fact that if I did not die prematurely old age would eventually force me to slow up. This was a predicament; I come from two long-lived families, my health was perfect, and I hated to be forced. So I slowed up voluntarily.

I made out a plan of living, the keynote of which was enjoyment, for if there is one thing I thoroughly believe in, it is to enjoy the twenty-four hours of the day if you can possibly swing it.

I had to keep housework and cooking in my schedule, for those things are my contribution toward keeping Fred and me alive. I couldn't cut them down to a minimum, for they had been down there all of our married life. One more tiny cut and Fred would divorce me. That I wouldn't like.

Writing? I didn't have to give that up, for all of my other work was physical and a change of occupation is rest.

Growing vegetables and flowers. Can't you see exactly where I would have been heading if I had not thought up mulching? Who can turn over a compost pile at the age of ninety? Not I —not even at the age of seventy, and I wouldn't have enjoyed it at fifty. And who could hoe and cultivate and weed a garden of any size at that age?

With benefit of mulching I have set myself a pleasant pace, which I can continue through my eighties if I don't break some bones. After ninety, from a wheeled chair if necessary.

I do everything myself; Mary and Virginia come to Poverty Hollow now for all-too-short visits. Besides the jobs I have mentioned I freeze a full winter's supply of vegetables and desserts (berries, peaches, sickle pears, plums) and make jam, pickles, relish and juices.

I have two rules: one is never to work after two o'clock in the afternoon except for a real emergency and to get dinner which, with a freezer to rely on, usually takes about twenty minutes. The other rule is never to do anything, even reading a novel or listening to music, unless I feel enthusiastic about it. I am almost always buoyant until after lunch; then I often begin to run downhill. When I get to the point where I don't feel enthusiastic about anything at all it means I'm sleepy, so I go and take a nap.

I see no reason why I can't keep up this rhythm indefinitely, never realizing that old age has arrived until some well-meaning friend calls me "spry." Then, of course, I will know where I belong, and will make an effort to act my age.

It is clear that if I had not stumbled onto mulching I would have had to give up the work I love best.

Since in the first chapters I emphasized the fact that I love to work in a garden, at first glance it may seem contradictory for me now to make a point of eliminating this work. At second glance it is clear enough. Those who want to spend the whole day in the garden still may, if they can spare the time, even with the new method. There will always be plenty of pleasant and interesting things to do there, fancy touches that one would never get around to if one gardened in the old-fashioned way.

But primarily I make a point of reducing the labor for those who are getting old, those who go to a job all day, for mothers with young children, and for those who do not like to garden but who want to have their own fresh vegetables and enjoy looking at flowers in their own yards.

And so, young or old, my friends, if for any reason you would like to grow things, throw away your spade and hoe and make your garden your compost pile. You will not be sorry, I promise you.

Love Will Find a Way

I AM GIVING STRAWBERRIES a chapter of their own because I have gone through so much with them, there is so much to tell. From the beginning they have been our best-loved crop, Fred's for eating, mine for growing.

Almost everyone I know who has a garden would like to grow them, but few of them do because they are so much work. I have good news for all such people: I have at last figured out an easy, effective way of growing strawberries which takes no more time or labor than any other crop.

The second spring I set out two rows of plants, 240 feet long. They were Premier (Howard 17). A neighbor gave them to me and it didn't occur to me to raise the question: were they the variety I wanted, the finest-flavored berry?

Nowadays, when somebody tells me he has put in some strawberry plants a neighbor has given him and I find that he doesn't know what kind they are, I am pained. Then I remind myself that, to the uninitiated, strawberries have no individuality, just as birds are merely birds to most city people.

Premier is handsome, sturdy and prolific. Accustomed as we were to store berries they tasted very good indeed. There were too many, of course; if you have never picked 480 feet of straw-berries, along with taking care of a giant-sized garden and doing your housework, you ought to try it, just to find out whether or not you are a superwoman.

Fred did what he could to help me get rid of them by eating a full quart three times a day. I sold some to the neighbors, made quantities of juice (like tomatoes, you can get rid of them faster if you drink them instead of eating them) and gave a lot away. Scott showed me how to make jam by putting berries and sugar in the sun under glass. The jam is delicious, but it is a slow process.

I sold a few crates to Dominick at a cruelly low price.

It was a tremendous lot of work. Virginia was in school during strawberry season and Mary was busy in New York. I went through all the elaborate routine: picked off hundreds of runners all summer long, made one new bed each year, but kept one old one, and weeded constantly. I mulched the plants when the berries began to set, to keep them clean, but I didn't know enough to keep them deeply mulched all the time to hold down the weeds. Earth for growing berries has to be very rich and weeds have a heyday if you don't forestall them.

The fourth year Rex told me there were berries with far better flavor than Premier; he was ordering some Fairfax, Catskill, and Dorsett and, if I wanted him to, he would have some sent to me. Naturally I wanted him to; another five hundred feet or so of berries was exactly what I needed to keep me out of mischief. But he was merciful and sent only twenty-five plants each of the three varieties.

Fairfax won the prize; it was far better than either Catskill or Dorsett. As for Premier, it should have been ashamed to show its pretty face in the same bed with Fairfax. But I didn't discard it because it bore so generously.

Even when I picked several crates of berries a day I never found the work tiresome or monotonous, probably because they were so beautiful. For eating, I prefer raspberries or cherries, but for the fun of growing and picking, give me strawberries, even Premier.

I liked every job connected with them. Your attitude to things you grow is like your attitude to people: you can enjoy any job, however much you may dislike it in itself, if it is for someone you love.

Ed Carlson had come back East again and spent a good deal of time in the barn during that summer when the raspberries produced so heavily that it was impossible to gather them all. He picked great quantities of them and reproached me because I wouldn't always help.

"You have an abnormal love for your strawberries," he scolded. "Kneeling over there, weeding next year's crop, while this year's raspberries are crying to be saved. You even like raspberries better, to eat. You ought to see a psychiatrist."

But he was in full sympathy with my love for picking them. Mary was, too; she always made a point of coming out in June to pick berries, partly to help me out, but partly because she loved the job. I have seen both her and Ed sitting on a cushion by a row of Catskill or Fairfax, getting great esthetic pleasure out of each individual berry, calling to me across the garden to come and admire a prize winner.

The third season after I started to grow the varieties which Rex had given me I had a crop failure of all except Premier. In my ignorance I didn't know what had happened; Art gave one look at the bed and told me that frost had killed the blossoms. It was only then that I found out that one reason for Premier's popularity was that it was frost-proof.

My real struggles against frost began. To protect most things —tomatoes, corn, beans, etc.—all you need to do is put them in late enough for safety. With strawberries you have no such simple solution. They are already planted; when they are ready to bloom, they bloom, and there is very little you can do about it. Oh, yes, you can keep the winter mulch on as late as you dare, but that doesn't make them blossom late enough to be safe, down here in the valley. I had had fine crops for two seasons without having done anything to protect them. Obviously that had been pure luck.

From that time on I kept hay piled all along the rows of berries during May and early June so that, if frost threatened, I could go out in the late afternoon and cover the plants. In the mornings I took it off. I hated to do it; I felt sure that all that putting on and pulling off of hay was bad for the blossoms not to mention being bad for me, with all I had to do.

There are days in the latter half of May and early June when the sun is bright and warm, but the air is cool, almost crisp. If you sit in the shade you might need a light wrap; you will surely need one if you sit in the house.

These are the rare days you have heard about; they are truly beautiful and are almost invariably followed by a chilly night. It is also likely to be a brilliant night, with a full moon.

Who doesn't love still, moonlit nights? Well, I don't always; I have found out how quietly cruel they can be.

A storm, a high wind, a hurricane may do a great deal of damage, but at least they are open and aboveboard about it. They are frankly in a rage and there is some excuse for their behavior. But a cold, moonlit night in May comes serenely smiling, seemingly in the best of humors, goes silently, still brilliantly smiling, and when it has gone, little live things lie black and dead. It is a casual, nonchalant kind of killing which is the most sinister of all.

Sometimes, by the end of May, I had dragged hay on and off the berry plants so often that I couldn't bear to do it again unless it was absolutely necessary. If there was a doubt about its freezing I would take a chance. Then, of course, I spent the evening watching the thermometer.

One of these times, by ten o'clock it was getting dangerously cold. It is a miserable task to cover the berries in the dark although we have done it more than once. So I decided to set the alarm for three o'clock and see how old Jack-you-know-who was progressing by then. Fred hated to have me take a chance on having to get up at three o'clock and do it then, and he knew I wouldn't call him. He wanted me to go with him to cover the plants, but I said no, and he couldn't go alone because he was too unfamiliar with the layout.

I was just falling asleep when I heard a tap on my door.

"Yes? What is it?" I asked.

"This is Lansing," a voice said. (This was a barn guest whom I hardly knew, a man who had a garden of his own; he had spent most of the day in the strawberry patch with me and knew exactly what was where.) "Turn off the alarm and go to sleep. I've covered the berries."

I haven't seen Lansing for many years, but I'll see him when I get to heaven; he'll be sitting right there on the right hand of God.

Another time, when at ten o'clock the thermometer said forty degrees, again Fred wanted to go out and help me cover the plants. I said, no, I was going to doze on the couch all night in my clothes and have a look at the thermometer every now and then. Fred accused me of being dramatic, but (although I know I have that failing) I don't think that was it. It was just too mean a job, in the dark, and if I could avoid it I was going to. So about once an hour I checked up; when at five o'clock it was only thirty-four degrees I went to bed for a while.

I was convinced by now that the severe cold crippled the berries even when it did not actually freeze them. Scott agreed with me and Fred made two movable cold frames, ten feet long, to put over the plants. If these did the trick he would make more, he said.

They did do the trick and Fred got John to build eight more of them. These second ones were only eight feet long, lighter and easier to handle than the first ones. Also, for these frames John made screens which could be put in when the berries began to ripen, to foil the birds. I used to have to almost give a catbird a push to make him get out of the way, so I could pick the berries. They are my favorite birds and I hated to defeat them in such a technical, man-thought-up way, so I often put a few berries on top of the screen for them. Don't think for a minute they don't find them.

These frames are a godsend. In early April we place them over the rows of berries and around four o'clock in the afternoon I close them.

To go back to our little friend Premier. One June we were expecting Lou and Dave Rasmussen for dinner. They were unusually fond of strawberries and knew good ones from those bought in the store. Some Premier were ripe; none of the others were. I picked a few boxes, ate one, made a face, and went to the cellar for some canned Fairfax. (This was before we had a freezer.)

That decided Premier's fate; if I preferred to serve canned Fairfax rather than fresh Premier why on earth was I fooling around with them? The frost was the reason (this was before Fred had built the frames), but even so I made up my mind to stop growing Premier.

Now I have permanent beds of Fairfax and Catskill and last spring I put in a few Empire. I would stick to Fairfax and nothing else, but they don't always come through as gloriously as they might and I feel that Catskill, which is thoroughly dependable and quite good, will do for jam and shortcakes for guests who wouldn't know the difference. We might even condescend to eat them for dessert ourselves, I suppose, if a season came when Fairfax went back on us altogether.

We haven't had a chance to taste Empire yet; it is a new berry and they say it is as dependable as Premier with a much finer flavor. If that turns out to be true I will continue to grow a few, they say it is an early berry and will give a longer season.

Selling berries was as much fun as playing store when we were youngsters, but one cannot have a silver lining without a cloud, it seems. On the dark side was the low price; I sold crates of berries to Dominick at eleven cents a box.

A whole crate of freshly picked strawberries is a beautiful sight and smells divine. It was a great pleasure to know that a lot of people were going to eat berries which were ripe when they were picked, a treat few people have an opportunity to enjoy.

Mary and I both got a great kick out of putting our strawberry sign on the post by the letter box and having people stop for them. Selling to the neighbors was routine (almost nobody grew them), but it was exciting when a stranger stopped, partly, I suppose, because no one ever failed to be impressed by the beauty of Catskill and the flavor of Fairfax. We put down the price of Premier and recommended them for jam only—which, as a matter of fact, was unfair to jam.

Here on the valley road not many strangers passed the house. It was quite a let-down if the fine sign Fred had made was out on its post and some stranger came in and asked the way to somebody's house instead of asking, how much are your berries?

One day a Mr. and Mrs. Grant stopped in. They were from Greenwich. I had just picked a lot of three kinds of berries and I put a number of boxes on the well top, for them to choose from. I noticed that one of the catbirds we had taught to take raisins from our hands was sitting on his accustomed branch waiting (patiently, for a change—usually he scolded) for me to hold out my hand with a raisin on it.

I always carried a few in my pocket (raisins, not catbirds) for at any moment a catbird might get hungry and pester me until I fed him. One of them followed Fred into the shop one day and sat there and scolded until Fred went to the house and got him some raisins.

Now, when I noticed the bird, somebody was talking and, absentmindedly, I put both a raisin and a berry on my hand and held it out toward the branch. If my mind had not been on something else I would have called their attention to the bird and would have given one of them the raisin. People find it exciting to have a bird light on their hand.

The little fellow swooped down and lit and just stood there on my upturned palm, looking the situation over. Usually he quickly took the raisin and flew away; he had never before been confronted with a choice. This time he could have either a berry or a raisin. He considered the matter and settled for both, ate the berry while sitting on my hand and then took the raisin and flew away.

My customers were speechless. If I had done it as we usually did when anyone was there to watch, made an exhibition of it, they would no doubt have been interested. But the casual way it had happened obviously made them feel that they had discovered a place where birds and people carried on little trans-actions with each other without question or exclamation. They came back all the way from Greenwich a number of times, for berries, they said, but I think they came to see the catbird.

When everything else doubled in price during the war years berries went away up too, but it was my bad luck that by that time I had calmed down considerably and was selling relatively few berries. Most of my customers could afford the high price, but there was one farmer down the road who had bought a box of berries every day for years while the season lasted and he couldn't afford to pay fancy prices. He knew a good berry when he tasted it and how he loved them!

I didn't dare put the price down for him (I had done it once, but he inadvertently told someone) because some of my other customers would have been annoyed; they were all friends or very friendly. I no longer grew Premier, which this man could have had at a lower price, and, anyway, I would have hated to sell him Premier. He loved Fairfax.

One day he stopped in (he bought only two or three boxes a week now) and suddenly I got a bright idea. I handed him a box of Fairfax and said: "These are only thirty cents. They're for jam."

He looked at them—there never was a handsomer sight—and then looked at me.

"They don't look like jam berries to me," he said.

"Well, they are and I'll have a box for you every day. But I won't have any for anyone else, so please don't spread it around."

He got up from his chair slowly—he was an old, tired, hard-working man—and said with a long, slow wink: "Well, I'll get along home and make some jam out of these. Pity they ain't fit to eat straight."

Not very long after that Fred bought a freezer and the selling days were over. Giving away days, too. A freezer reveals your true nature; my generosity went right down to zero.

Since I am not blind, I naturally came to know the different varieties of strawberries by sight as well as by taste. Anyone

who happened to see me rescue a Fairfax from a box of Catskill
where it had landed by mistake was surprised and impressed.
They were as surprised as I had been when I came out of Kansas
before the days of radio and the opportunity to hear good music
and had met people who could tell a composer by the style of the
music, even when they were not familiar with that particular
piece. It was a result of their familiarity with the art, though
I had thought it was a great gift one had to be born with.

I have never been able to figure out why strawberries occupy
such a special place in the fruit world. For instance, it is February, you are expecting some company you want to impress
and you haven't time to make a cherry pie, or biscuit tortoni,
or to attempt that elaborate recipe for Supreme Something-or-
other you have never yet had the courage to tackle. So you buy a
miserable, tasteless box of strawberries (don't shop around,
they are all terrible), wash, stem, sweeten, and chill the wretched
things and your guests will exclaim: "Ah-h-h! Fresh strawberries!" And seem to enjoy them.

They certainly are not much good, so why is this? Did it
just get started, like the unreasoning and unreasonable hate
and fear of nonpoisonous snakes? Got started and kept on
gathering momentum?

Yet, with all of this overbalanced enthusiasm for any old
kind of strawberries, very few people grow them. Everyone
says they are too much work.

And they are. Whether you put in a new bed each year or
use two- or three-year-old ones, you have quite a job on your
hands. Transplanting is work, and even if you mulch to keep
down the weeds, you still have the fussy, time-consuming job
of controlling and spacing the runners.

At long last I have worked out an easy, efficient, satisfactory
way of growing strawberries, which does away with almost all
of the work.

First, I make sure to choose a spot where I want my strawberry bed to be, forever, for this is as permanent as asparagus.
You do it only once.

I planted three rows of plants, the rows about six inches apart

—planted so closely, this actually means one row, three plants abreast.

I permitted the first plant in each row to make only one runner, straight down the row, and let all other plants in each row make two runners, one up, one down the row. When I was finished I had three rows of plants, the rows six inches apart, the plants in each row one foot apart. But it looks like, and is, actually, one row of berries.

I put mine in in October, since I greatly prefer fall planting. A year from the following spring, after I had picked the first crop, I pulled up the first plant in each of the three rows, left plants number two and three, pulled up number four, left five and six, and so on. In other words I got rid of the mother plants and left the plants that had been made by their runners. Then, during that summer, the plants I had kept were allowed to make just enough runners to replace the ones I had pulled up. Year after year the older plants are removed, the newer ones are kept, and that is not much of a job.

You now have a permanent bed of strawberries, part of which is always in its first year, part in its second year. You will never have to transplant again unless you wish to try a new variety. New ones are coming out all the time and one is often tempted. You have to control the runners, but there is a tremendous difference between placing, exactly, only one or two runners to each plant and the old system of placing a number of them rather haphazardly.

If the bed is kept well mulched it will have no weeds. If you have not yet graduated from the hard work of a compost pile you can give each new plant a handful of that earth, if you feel it is necessary. Or manure, if you use it.

Since I use neither manure nor chemical fertilizer I let the ever-rotting mulch do the job. I also give the plants some wood ashes, but I am not convinced that it is particularly helpful. I wouldn't give it a second thought if I didn't have any. If I should ever feel that the plants needed it I would give them some of my kind of compost—the unbelievably rich dirt between the rows of asparagus, which has been made through the years by rotting mulch. In August when, I have been told, the plants make their buds for the following year, I treat them to a little cotton seed meal, for nitrogen.

I think my ground is now so rich from rotted mulch that I could get away with planting more closely, and I will probably try it some day.

There seems to be differences of opinion among the experts about when to put on the winter mulch. Some say to do it just before the thermometer drops to twenty degrees above zero; others say to wait until the ground is frozen hard. They agree that you must not put it on heavily too early.

I wrote to W. F. Allen Co., strawberry growers in Maryland, some years ago, and asked their advice. I knew that they recommended the twenty-degrees method, but that was a little too uncertain for my comfort. How could I know, when I went to bed, what the thermometer might decide to do at 2 A.M.? And yet I must not cover the berries too soon.

I asked Mr. Allen how it would be if I gave the plants a very light covering of hay sometime in early November, so light that even if the weather got quite warm again it would not injure the plants, and yet sufficient to protect them if the temperature went down to twenty; then, later, when the ground became solidly frozen, to pile hay on thickly, keeping the earth frozen, if possible, until time to take off the mulch.

He wrote back that that would be ideal if I was willing to take the time. I have done that for years and it doesn't take much extra time for, when I put on the first light covering, I pile the hay I am going to use later all along the row, ready to toss on when the ground is frozen hard.

When I uncover the plants in spring I always check up to make sure that thawing and freezing has not loosened the roots. This is not nearly as much of a job as it used to be for with this new way of growing berries the plants are uniform and easy to get at.

One word about everbearers: phooey! No, a few more words:

first, they will not produce for me and, second, the people I know who grow them have never, in my presence, had enough to serve, although they do rush in from the patch with five, or maybe even six, berries in their hand, gloating: "Look! Strawberries out of the patch at this time of year!"

If everbearers are a success commercially, why don't we see them in market in the autumn? I never have. I had an article about strawberries published recently and received a letter from Allan Field, in New Jersey, who had read it. He says: "I have also experimented with everbearers, but, like everyone else, I have met with no success."

Later, Mrs. Mary Goebel, in Oregon, wrote saying that she does have good luck with everbearers and that one sees them in the market out there. Strawberries are well known for their capacity for drinking, and Fred says that Oregon is well known for its frequent rains. Could our stingy clouds be the reason for our failure to grow everbearers?

But who cares that fresh strawberries in winter are pretty awful and everbearers seemingly almost nonexistent, if you can open your freezer and take out a container of last spring's delicious crop, looking forward to another June with its lovely gift of fresh Fairfax?

Enemy Aliens

WOODCHUCKS, CUTWORMS, MEXICAN BEETLES and all such de-spoilers ought to be in a book by themselves; they should not be allowed to contaminate any subject as pleasant as gardening. But they contaminate the garden itself and therefore, unfortunately, they belong here.

I dislike woodchucks intensely and it is not only because they eat up my vegetables. Rabbits are destructive, too, and yet I'm very fond of them. I can't help liking their impudence. If a woodchuck sees you coming he scurries off through the corn patch, but a rabbit will look at you in a friendly, companionable way and, as often as not, will take another helping of lettuce before deciding that, for the moment, he has had enough.

As for deer, I feel more flattered than pained when they nibble the asparagus. That is, if they don't make a habit of it. Flattery is pleasing only in small doses.

A woodchuck is extremely distasteful to me; it reminds me of an ugly woman in a mangy fur coat who has spent the night in a gutter. Not that I blame the poor woman any more than I blame the woodchuck, but there is certainly nothing attractive about either one of them, as there is about a rabbit or a deer. Or a pretty woman in a new mink.

I have fought these miserable, unblamable creatures for twenty-five years. Up to a point I have at last outsmarted them.

Many people believe that a fence, if you dig a trench and put it down several inches, is the answer. I don't know. Only last summer two acquaintances of mine with fences like that complained that woodchucks had got into the garden, and they insisted that there was no opening, nothing to show how they had managed it. They were convinced that the intruders had climbed the fence.

It seemed to me a tremendous job for anyone to have to dig a trench all around my big garden. But to fence off only the things that attracted woodchucks and rabbits wasn't practical for I was told that crops should be rotated. If I did that the fence would not always be protecting the necessary things.

Other people think you should hunt up the woodchuck holes and treat them with poison gas. Fred tried that for a season or two, but it didn't seem to answer. We have acres of meadow; Fred found thirty-five holes, but if he missed just one he might better have saved his time and money. One woodchuck can clean up the garden in one night if the plants are young. A number of our neighbors who used that method still had woodchuck trouble.

Fred shot a good many of the creatures (one season he got fourteen) and so did any other man who happened to be staying in the barn if he liked to use a gun. At that time I was a vegetarian and it surprised and pained one of my friends, Susan Townsend, when I would run to Fred and ask him to get the gun. She was an artist, a tenderhearted, gentle girl and she would protest: "Ruth, how can you want anything killed just because it eats a few vegetables? You always have plenty; they don't take everything."

I would give her some kind of inadequate answer and we would go through that same dialogue each time I called for the gun. Susan spent all of her summers in the barn loft and so, poor girl, she saw, or rather heard, a lot of killing.

She seldom did anything in the vegetable garden. When she wanted a job she preferred to help Mother weed the flower beds. But one day I was faced with six dozen plants to set out; she knew I didn't like transplanting so she offered to help me.

Then came a dry spell, and for several days Susan and I carried water out to our little plants to keep them alive. A few weeks went by and they seemed to enjoy growing rapidly to repay us for all our trouble.

One morning I went out and saw the disaster: almost every one of them was eaten. They were so young there wasn't much more than a bite in each so the enemy had gone right up and down all the rows.

I went to the barn in search of someone to share my sorrow and ran into Susan.

"You just ought to see—it's worth looking at," I told her. "Come on, I'll show you something."

She went with me to the garden, looked at the devastated area, and said: "It's too bad, but you have so many things they don't eat. You still have—"

Her face changed suddenly, her eyes got big, her mouth opened wide and she gasped: "Ruth! Why, those are the little plants we put out and watered and worked so hard to keep alive. Where's Fred? Did you see the woodchuck? Has he gone?"

"He's gone," I said bitterly, "and so are the plants. They were eaten too clean, they can't possibly come back. And it's too late in the season to put in any more."

Susan put her arm around me.

"Now I understand. It's the work and the love you put into it. It's as if they kept chewing up my paintings. I never realized—"

Yes, it was that and something more. It was also the old, old story of unfulfillment, premature death. True, through me the woodchucks had also died a premature death whenever I could swing it. But human beings are so constituted (unfortunately, perhaps) that the death of an enemy does not disturb them unduly.

In my battle against these marauders I did one clumsy, inadequate thing after another. I tried covering the vegetables they liked best (soy beans, kohlrabi and beet tops) with bushel baskets and any other thing I could lay my hands on, but then they settled for what they liked second best. There were hardly enough baskets in the state of Connecticut to cover everything.

It was a nuisance, too, to do all that covering each night and uncovering in the morning. One blustery, rainy night I skipped it, telling myself that in such weather they would all surely stay at home where they belonged. The next morning I found to my disgust that woodchucks and rabbits were like postmen: "Neither snow nor rain nor heat nor gloom of night stays these couriers from the swift completion of their appointed rounds."

If you go to a job every morning in the city the likelihood of running into a surprise when you arrive is small. Fire and theft are the only two things I can think of offhand that could have changed things overnight, and they happen rarely. There is no such monotony in the country.

Quite aside from disasters, such as woodchucks, frosts, and high winds, there are innumerable small and pleasant changes. A fine crop of asparagus this morning; many berries ripening overnight; heads of cauliflower starting which surely weren't there yesterday; a few peppers beginning to show color. Possibly a steady gentle rain through the night has made both gardens, flower and vegetable, look like a crowd of bright, eager children with freshly washed faces. There is chance of heartache and headache for a gardener, but no chance of boredom.

Finally, I thought up a scheme for protecting the vegetables against woodchucks, and Fred agreed that it might work. He built eight cages for me out of chicken wire. They were open on one long side and were ten feet long, three feet high and three feet wide. They were light in weight and fairly easy to handle and I put them over the rows of vegetables that tempted woodchucks and rabbits. They were so wide that I could plant two rows of things such as lettuce, beets, kohlrabi under one frame.

Most people who saw the cages thought the animals would go right under them. They didn't for a long time; I think it was six years before something got the bright idea to crawl under and eat the kohlrabi.

The frames are twelve years old now and half of them are

sort of falling apart. After we got the movable, strawberry cold frames there was no space for housing the cages in winter and they've been through some ice storms and a hurricane or two.

Here is a trick John taught me last summer and it worked. A woodchuck had got in the garden one night, and the next morning I told John about it. He looked around and found the path through the grass and weeds where the thief had made a beeline for the cabbage.

He took two of the wire cages and placed them in such a position that if the woodchuck came along his previous path there would be just enough room for him to get into the garden between the two cages. Then John took the trap, not even bothering to bait it, and set it in that opening. He told me the woodchuck would probably walk right into the open trap.

I was skeptical for it was late in the season and when things are full grown I get careless about barricades. There were plenty of safe ways for the beast to get to the cabbage. But John was right. The next morning when I went out to investigate there was a perfectly huge woodchuck in the trap, looking disgusted and furious—not even a bite of a carrot to compensate for his tough luck.

This year I am trying something new. I got two big loads of spoiled hay from Art in the spring and made a wall of hay on each end of the garden instead of leaving it in one big pile. This will be handy when I want a few pitchforks of mulch and, also, I am convinced that it will nonplus the woodchucks. On each side of the garden is a row of strawberries with movable cold frames which no animal has ever yet dared to climb over, apparently, although I am sure they could. And we will always keep the trap handy in case we need it.

I want to take a minute to tell the story about the Sunday when I went out to pick some corn for dinner and saw there was a skunk in the trap. Fred kills the woodchucks by putting the trap into a box he made for that purpose. It has only a small hole to take the hose from the exhaust of the automobile and this is a quick and painless death.

But a skunk was a different matter; Fred wouldn't kill a gentle, harmless skunk and I certainly wouldn't want him to. He has often walked quietly up to the trap when a skunk was in it and let him out. It seems that skunks are conscious of their powerful defense and are therefore relatively fearless. Fred has found that if he approaches them quietly they don't use their weapon against him. And they give you warning; if they become nervous or irritated they begin treading with their front feet, which means you had better run.

This day it was not going to be so easy because a neighbor's dog had spied the trap and was barking and carrying on and the skunk was upset. Fred was wondering what to do when our dinner guests, Than and Alma Selleck, drove in. Than is our doctor and Fred asked him if he had his bag with him. He had, so he and Fred put some morphine into a tempting tidbit of something or other, put it on the end of a long stick and fed it to the skunk. The little fellow went peacefully to sleep, Fred opened the cage door, and when the skunk woke up he walked out. Now Fred has fixed the trap with a long string so that he can open it from a safe distance if such a thing happens again.

My second least-loved pest is the mole. Almost invariably they choose one of my favorite crops to undermine. Once in an age a mole trap catches one and it is possible that moth balls and the like dispose of them. The trouble is you seldom know.

Most of the people around here have their tulip bulbs eaten by moles. They have never bothered mine. If they did, first I think I would try planting garlic in the tulip bed. I read in the *Rural New Yorker* that that absolutely drives them away. Then the question arises: where does it drive them to? The strawberry patch? If the garlic didn't work I suppose I would line the tulip bed with wire. A big job, but effective.

I have gone down a long row of strawberries on my knees, following a mole run with my fingers, gently feeling under the plants, pressing the earth back around the roots. It is a long tedious job, but has to be done if a mole has been there and you want to save your plants. Simply killing the little monster, assuming you can, does not remedy the damage he has already done.

You can go along for years without any mole trouble at all and then all of a sudden they will be driving you crazy. After quite a long interlude, this past summer they built an intricate subway system under our lawn. But at least in a lawn you notice them at once, while they can be in the asparagus bed for quite a long time before you discover them.

Cumbersome and inadequate as it sounds and is, I know no effective way to protect your garden from moles except to keep an eye open and, if a row of something begins to look distressed, get down on your knees—no, don't pray, look for a mole run. If you find one, follow it along its full length, pressing the earth back in place.

Nobody else seems to have the final answer, either, for one constantly runs across items saying, "Now we've found out how to control moles." If there was a satisfactory solution to the problem people would not be constantly thinking up new ones.

The *Garden Encyclopedia* says that moles may be benefiting you more than they are harming you; that if you have lots of moles it may be because you have lots of insects. This may explain why I have seen no moles in the garden since I've been mulching it and also explain why I have never had them at all in the row of tulips. I have always mulched the tulips.

Cutworms are repulsive little fat worms which usually cut a young plant off just above the surface of the earth. They take a bit of nourishment from it and leave the rest of it lying there. Then they go on to the next plant. If they were considerate enough to eat the whole thing and leave some of the other plants for you, you wouldn't get so annoyed at them.

For a year or two I went through the routine of scattering poisoned bran all over the garden. It was effective, but I didn't like the job so I began using paper collars. You take a six-inch piece of paper and put it around each plant, half below the surface of the ground, half above, wrapping it securely around the stem of the plant, holding the paper in place by making the earth firm around it. A job, but you do it only once a season and it saves your plants. Now that I am mulching everything I never take any precautions and I never see a cutworm.

Mexican beetles had me completely stymied during the premulching era. I can't explain why it was, but, somehow, I was always making my spray too strong, which burned the leaves of the beans. The plants were yellow with beetles and what a treat it is now never to see one!

The pests and diseases that are said to threaten tomatoes never upset me for I automatically sprayed the plants according to directions and had good luck. Now, since I mulch everything, I never spray the plants and have healthy vines and splendid crops.

Like everyone else I had my fun with Japanese beetles. They are pretty if you can look at them objectively, but who can?

That first year when they invaded the valley I bought dollars worth of mosquito netting and tried to put it over the red raspberry bushes because the berries had already formed and we couldn't spray them. (Curiously enough, there was not a beetle on the black raspberries.) It was quite impossible to cover a lot of tall raspberry bushes effectively; some way or other the wretches found their way under the netting.

I deserted the pole beans entirely; the Japanese beetles were so thick on them you could scarcely see a bean. I saved myself from nausea by avoiding that end of the garden. Cal Kallgren gave me some of the traps people were using and we caught a few million beetles in them. A drop in the bucket.

I cut the roses the minute they showed any color and put halves of yellow canteloupes (which I read was effective for attracting the beetles) under the rosebushes. It wasn't effective.

The following year I gave up the mosquito netting, put some kerosene in a tin can, and spent the summer, more or less, picking beetles off raspberries, roses, zinnias and numerous other things, throwing them into the can. I never became skillful at that; I was so afraid the beast would escape on its journey from my fingers to the kerosene that I threw it in violently, often splashing it, and my hair smelled of kerosene all summer although I was constantly washing it. It was a nightmare. Toward the end of August I threw away the can, defeated.

Mary asked me: "Don't you hate them enough by now so that you can just pick them off and squash them?"

I found that I did.

Then Art told me about lime. If you cover a bush with lime or anything white (flour will do) the beetles won't go near it, he said. I tried it and he was right.

Of course, that doesn't kill the beetles and you have to repeat it after every rain. Also, the roses and zinnias aren't very pretty covered with lime and you have to wash the raspberries thoroughly to get it off, whereas raspberries are so delicate they should not be washed at all. And needn't be—if you grow them yourself and pick them carefully.

Many things fresh from the garden should not be washed. Berries of all kinds are much better off not, and if you are willing to eat a handful which the gardener gives you out in the patch it is inconsistent to feel fastidious about it if she serves them unwashed for dessert. A little trust is all you have to have, and not nearly as much of that as you need every time you eat a meal in a restaurant.

Then we heard that Japanese beetles breed in lawns and, if you had your lawn soaked with D.D.T. just once, the beetles would get progressively fewer and fewer through the years. It was important, however, for your neighbors to do it too. We persuaded all the valley people to treat their lawns and the beetles have dwindled to almost none. Last summer we had six. Six beetles, I mean, not six billion.

I am not saying that the soaking with D.D.T. is the only reason the beetles have disappeared. I am told that birds are cultivating a taste for Japanese beetles and that the problem is being solved by them.

I am so grateful to be rid of them that I don't particularly care what the reason is. I am no longer a vegetarian, but I never criticized a bird for eating a bug or worm even when I was. But I am particularly fond of catbirds and I do hope they have not formed the habit of eating Japanese beetles, which are far too repulsive to eat. Besides, I can't get rid of the feeling that they all smell and taste like kerosene.

If you live in an ivory tower you can have perfectly charming thoughts about the oneness of all life and about putting a fly out of doors rather than killing it. That kind of sentiment appeals to me.

I don't like to see the strong take advantage of the weak. I have some kind of vague distaste for man using his superior skill and brains to make instruments and weapons against which a mere little animal is helpless. I dislike killing or violence of any kind. I don't like birds eating worms, cats killing birds, or men killing everything, including each other.

And yet I kill. I kill a mosquito with satisfaction if it is buzzing and biting me, a fly almost with indifference, a cutworm with disgust. For anything bigger than that I call Fred, who is kinder, but braver, than I am.

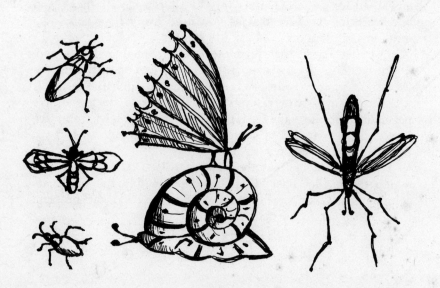

Which Shall It Be?

THIS CHAPTER IS AN ALPHABETICAL LIST of the varieties of vegetables I am ordering for the coming season. With few exceptions, which I mention, they are the ones I have been growing for many years. If you decide to use this list as a guide, bear in mind that in almost every case I grow the vegetable I believe to have the finest flavor, rather than for other desirable characteristics.

Also, with each vegetable named I give my experience in freezing it.

My list is made up from Joseph Harris and Company's catalog; if you have a favorite seedman you will no doubt find most of these varieties listed in his catalog.

ASPARAGUS.—I cannot do anything for you about this for I bought my roots twenty-four years ago and apparently better kinds have been developed since then.

It freezes so well that, in the spring, when I pass from frozen to fresh asparagus, Fred doesn't even know it although he is extremely asparagus-conscious. And let me say here, do not judge home-frozen vegetables by commercially frozen ones. The former are invariably superior—at least mine are, and I am not conceited enough to think that I am better at it than anybody else.

BEANS.—In order to get an early crop I grow a ten-foot row of bush beans. When they run their course the pole beans, planted at the same time, begin to produce, and from then on we get beans until frost. If you plant both bush and pole varieties you are saved the bother of making new plantings through the summer. Also, pole beans are prolific, delicious, and take little space.

For bush beans, lately, I have been planting *Wade*. The catalog calls it a "truly great variety." "Great" is a somewhat elaborate word to use for a bean, but its flavor is excellent and it is productive. You will notice that *Topcrop* is listed as an early bean and *Wade* as a midseason one, but you will also see that there are only four days' difference in the times of maturing. Unless you are so eager for beans that you cannot wait four more days you need plant only *Wade*. Just now, though, I received the 1955 catalog and *Improved Tendergreen* sounds so tempting I may order those this year instead of *Wade*.

If you want to grow wax (yellow) beans, *Pencil Pod Black Wax* is the best. In my experience wax beans are much less prolific than the green ones and I no longer grow them.

I like *Scotia* very much for a pole bean, but I notice the catalog says that *Kentucky Wonder* is excellent for freezing, but doesn't say a word about freezing *Scotia,* so I am going back to *Kentucky Wonder*.

I was never able to get a satisfactory crop of lima beans until a few years ago when Harris began to sell treated seed. Before that my season was too short, for when the seed was not treated it was necessary to put off planting until about June tenth to avoid rotting in cold, damp weather and to guard against corn-maggot injury. Now I grow *Fordhook U. S. 242* treated seed and get fair crops. The season here in the valley is still too short for a bumper crop of limas. I "cover the limas with apple blossoms," as they tell you to do with corn, meaning: plant your corn when the apple blossoms begin to fall.

I have never grown pole limas, again because of the short season, but next year, with treated seed, I am going to put in a few poles, plant the seeds early in May under hotkaps (waxed paper cones) and try my luck. *Ideal Pole Lima* is the only kind Harris lists, saying it is so superior that they do not handle any other variety. Lima beans freeze perfectly.

I tried *Horticultural* twice and its flavor was the finest I have ever tasted in any bean. But those were my pre-mulching days; I was very busy, they didn't produce satisfactorily and they were too much work for the little I got out of them. I am going to try *French Horticultural* again next spring, now that my mulching system gives me so much free time.

I also grow soy beans, *Bansei*, which we think are fully as delicious as the best lima. Harris doesn't carry them; you'll have to get them from somebody else. They freeze perfectly.

Many people say they don't care for frozen string beans, even home frozen. Try this: Cook them as you would if you were going to eat them at once, being careful not to get them too soft. Cool gradually and freeze. When you take them from the freezer thaw them slowly, then either heat them or make a salad of them.

BEETS.—For years I have stuck to *Detroit Dark Red* for the summer beet and *Long Season* for the winter one. However, with a freezer one does not need to grow a winter beet and I don't quite know why I do.

Most people will tell you that beets don't freeze satisfactorily, but if you ignore the freezing rules, cook your beets as if you were going to have them for dinner, let them stand until they are cool, then put them in the freezer, you will find them just as good when you take them out as when you put them in. I usually freeze beets and beans by cooking two or three times too many for dinner and freezing what is left over. You can also freeze Harvard and pickled beets satisfactorily.

BROCCOLI.—I always planted *Italian Green Sprouting* until last summer when I tried the new *Waltham 29*. Both are fine. If you freeze broccoli it is important to have it solid and young. Then it freezes perfectly.

CABBAGE.—I don't grow early cabbage from seed; John does and gives me some plants. For late cabbage John grows *Bugner* and I grow *Harris' Special Strain of Danish Ballhead* and we exchange plants. I like Savoy cabbage and grow *Vanguard*. It is a beautiful thing to look at. Some day I am going to put a head of Savoy cabbage right in the middle of a flower bed and listen to the comments. If you want red cabbage, *Red Danish.*

Both coleslaw and cooked cabbage freeze pretty satisfactorily, but John has persuaded me to stop crowding the freezer with it. He lays it in the garden and tosses some hay on it. I did that, just this morning. The hay must be about waist high and must slope so the rain will run off.

CARROTS.—I like both *Nantes* and *Tendersweet* so much that I am never tempted by another variety. Since I've been mulching, mine get huge and yet stay crisp, tender and sweet.

Carrots freeze well. Like beets and beans, one good way is to cook them until they are tender (not too soft), cool slowly and freeze. Then you can use them for stew, salad or buttered carrots.

CAULIFLOWER: SNOWBALL IMPERIAL.—I get very fine large heads with no trouble at all since I have been mulching. I also grow purple cauliflower, *New Early Purple Head.* Do you know it? It behaves like cauliflower (of course you don't bleach it), but we think it tastes like broccoli. The heads grow to an immense size and are a deep, lovely purple. A friend saw mine for the first time last fall and exclaimed: "How perfectly beautiful! What do you do with them? Wear them in your hair?"

Cauliflower freezes perfectly and comes through as white as snow if you do it when it is in its prime.

CHINESE CABBAGE: MICHIHLI.—This is nice to have, say on Thanksgiving, when there is nothing else green to serve raw and fresh from the garden. You can neglect thinning part of it and cook it for greens. I have frozen the cooked greens with good results.

COLLARDS: VATES.—You can have collards from spring right into winter. Cook them slowly for a long time with a piece of salt pork and/or smoked bacon rind. Very good, and what is left over goes into the freezer.

CORN.—For early corn *Sun Up* is very good and so is *North Star.* And *Miniature* is unbelievably sweet. I find it hard to decide which of these three to grow for the early crop; sometimes I plant a little of each. For the second crop comes *Carmelcross.*

Five days later there is *Hoosier Gold,* but for the home garden
you can skip from *Carmelcross* to the main crop. I have grown
only *Golden Cross Bantam* for many years for this crop, but so
many people are praising *Iochief* that John and I are going to
try a little next summer. And now the 1955 catalog is here and
I am deserting *Golden Cross Bantam* in favor of *Wonderful,*
a new Harris corn which they are simply raving about. It is
real proof of my faith in what Harris says about his vegetables
that I fearlessly order a half pound of *Wonderful* and only
a packet of *Golden Cross Bantam,* for corn is a crop I would
hate badly to go wrong on.

Corn freezes beautifully if you pick it when it is exactly
right, not a minute too young, not a second too old. Pick just
enough at a time to pop it all right into the steamer, leave it on
the cob or cut it off, and you have something truly delicious.
The consistency is never as crisp as that of fresh corn, but the
flavor is there.

CUCUMBERS.—I like *Marketer. China* is fun to grow and so
is *Lemon,* for novelties. For pickling, *Harris' Double Yield* is fine.

DANDELION.—Go out on the lawn and help yourself. I did
grow them in the garden, though, one year, when I was a little
crazier than I am now.

DILL: LONG ISLAND MAMMOTH.—It seeds itself adequately,
but if you mulch, it is simpler to plant it each year.

HERBS.—I have two fine tarragon bushes, a bed of thyme,
chives, and a sage bush. And dill—I could hardly keep house
without dill for salads, soups, sauces and many other things.

KALE.—John gives me plants.

KOHLRABI: EARLY WHITE VIENNA.—We like this raw, or as
salad, or in stews. I freeze it thoroughly cooked, not too soft,
ready to make a salad.

LEEKS.—I settle for onions.

LETTUCE.—*Great Lakes* is far and away my favorite, but I
am afraid that is largely because it is so impressive. Since the
mulching began the heads are tremendous and beautiful. I also
have been growing *Mignonette* because it is earlier than *Great*

Lakes. Salad Bowl, which has been almost hysterically popular, is most satisfactory as a producer. I gave it up because I like a lettuce which is dark green, one of the charms of *Great Lakes.* But I like what the 1955 catalog says about *Matchless* and I am going to try it next spring instead of *Mignonette.*

ONIONS.—The variety in choosing sets or seeds is a matter of personal taste: do you want yellow ones or white ones? I plant *Ebenezer* sets, which are yellow. I plant *Sweet Spanish* seeds; in a good season I get fine large onions. But the prize comes from the *Sweet Spanish* plants. Since the mulching days began we get remarkably sweet onions, many of them weighing a pound and a half apiece.

I have heard that onions freeze well, raw, but I see no point in freezing them. They keep perfectly, right there in the bin.

PARSLEY: PARAMOUNT.—You can freeze it very easily; one way is to grind it and put, say, a quarter or half cup of it into an ordinary envelope, seal it and stick it into the freezer. That way it takes up little room.

PARSNIPS: HARRIS' MODEL.—Since I've been mulching mine are much finer and larger than they were previously.

PEAS: LINCOLN.—I have already exhausted the subject of peas in a previous chapter. I also grow both bush and climbing *Edible Pod Peas.* Harris doesn't carry them; I think I ordered them from Burgess last year. You eat the pod before the peas form. Fred prefers them to regular peas.

Both kinds of peas are excellent frozen.

PEPPERS.—I buy *Vinedale* seeds and get Frank Mead, in Bethel, to start them for me. I do this because *Vinedale* turns red in our short season. I also buy a few bull nose plants from Mr. Mead. However, I just now noticed that Harris calls *Penn-wonder* the finest early pepper, so this year I'll try both and see which I prefer.

Peppers freeze beautifully raw. Just take out the seeds and cut them in half or leave them whole, as you prefer. There is one difficulty: if you freeze them whole when they are bright red they are so beautiful that you can hardly bring yourself to eat them. It's like shooting a deer.

PUMPKINS.—I grow *Small Sugar*. If you cook too much to eat up, it freezes perfectly, either straight or made up ready for pies.

RADISHES.—We prefer the white *Icicle* to the red ones although I grow a few *Cherry Belle* because red ones are earlier than the white and we are always eager for the first radish.

RASPBERRIES.—I am growing *September*, an everbearing variety, and I wish I had put in *Taylor*. Our autumn frosts come too early for an everbearer; the berries freeze before they ripen. Probably I'll change to *Taylor* some day.

Raspberries freeze beautifully.

RHUBARB: MACDONALD.—It is both handsome and tender and freezes perfectly.

SPINACH.—I grow both *America* and *Viking* because I have never been able to make up my mind which I prefer. I also usually buy a packet of *Blight Resistant Savoy* for fall planting although I don't have much luck with fall spinach. I think it is because my enthusiasm for growing things is at its lowest ebb in September. Sometimes I even forget to put in the fall spinach.

Spinach freezes perfectly; I steam it until it barely begins to get soft, cool quickly in icy water, and freeze.

SQUASH.—Our summer squash is *Harris' Hybrid Cocozelle*. We usually eat them raw, picking them when they are about as big as a medium-sized cucumber. Art eats them like an apple and knows just where to go to find one in my garden. I serve them with salad dressing, either alone or combined with cucumbers, tomatoes, lettuce, spinach, or milkweed, if I can find some. Nothing improves a salad more than the top leaves of a milkweed plant.

For winter squash I grow *Butternut* and *Blue Hubbard*. *Butternut* is easier to handle, but we think *Blue Hubbard* has the finest flavor of any squash. Besides, it is too beautiful to miss. If you want you can cut a piece off one just big enough for dinner and keep the rest for quite awhile, but I usually cook the whole squash and freeze what is left over. *Blue Hubbard* is so big that one is enough to last us all winter; the others I give away.

I always freeze squash by cooking and mashing it, ready to eat.

TOMATOES.—I greatly prefer the flavor of *Pink Ponderosa* to that of any other variety, but it is erratic. It cheerfully ignores the traditions and customs. Once in awhile it conforms and offers you a conventional, round tomato, but usually *Pink Ponderosa* makes me think of some of the modern painters: they are going to be different, by heck, no matter how grotesque the outcome. And so I also grow a few *Rutgers*. I can't fully trust *Pink Ponderosa;* one fine day they might decide it would be good fun not to produce anything at all. I grow *Red Cherry* tomatoes, too; they are pretty, delicious, handy, and make a great hit with children.

The freezer is always so crowded and canning tomatoes is so easy that I have never tried freezing them. I hear that one can do so for stewing or juice, but not for salad, of course.

TURNIPS.—I grow both *Purple-Top White Globe* and *Golden Ball.* I would not want to be without a white turnip, but I grow a few *Golden Ball* because they are so round and attractive. I also grow *Alta Sweet* rutabaga.

Turnips freeze satisfactorily if you would rather do that than keep them under hay or in a root cellar.

Early in January when I settle myself on the couch before a crackling fire with the new catalog, pen and paper, ready to order the seeds for the coming season, I usually think: This year I'll experiment a little. I am in a rut, planting more or less the same varieties every year.

I come out the way I do when I go to a party and think I'll look around for new and different people to talk to and get acquainted with, and maybe make some new friends. First thing

I know I am in a corner with some old pal, tried and true, too satisfied with what I have to look around for something better, or even something additional. I do not necessarily approve of this, in regard to either vegetables or people, but I am afraid I will have to think worse of it than I do now before I make a serious effort to change.

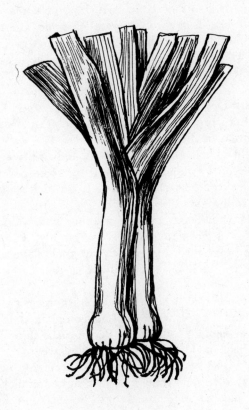

Easy Does It

THIS CHAPTER IS AN ATTEMPT to make gardening easier for you in various small ways. If you are a seasoned gardener I am sure you have shortcuts of your own, but there may be some here you have not thought of. Some of mine are the result of using my head instead of the strength I haven't got.

Again we will start alphabetically, putting the miscellaneous suggestions after the ones for each vegetable.

ASPARAGUS.—Don't cut it off under the ground with an asparagus cutter; break it at whatever point it snaps easily. This saves a great deal of time.

We are told to harvest asparagus for only six weeks. I like to stop a little sooner than that; then, if for some reason I want to serve it, the seventh or eighth week I can pick some without feeling I am robbing the bed.

You have to pick it every day whether you want to eat it then or not for it goes to seed very promptly. Put it in the refrigerator and save it for tomorrow (but you'll have some more tomorrow) or freeze it or give it away or sell it, but at least pick it.

Don't rob the cradle. I helped Dave Rasmussen put in a bed of asparagus and two years later Lou complained to me that there was never enough for a meal. Because she liked asparagus tips she had been picking them when they weren't more than two inches high. Give it a chance—six or eight inches; you will soon be able to tell when it is just right for picking.

BEANS.—I haven't enough strength to make a hole deep

enough for a pole by using a crow bar. So, first I shovel out some earth; then I take the crow bar and make a small hole in the center of the big one I've made. I put in the pole, pull back the earth and have a good firm job. Of course, I cut the poles in midwinter when there is little else I can do out of doors to get some fresh air and exercise.

Because bush beans are an early-harvested crop I plant a few cabbage plants right in the same row with them. When I pull the bean plants out the cabbage has everything its own way.

BEETS.—If you like beet tops don't thin the beets until they are big enough to use the surplus plants for greens. You can transplant beets if you want to. (See lettuce for early planting.)

BROCCOLI.—This is no original trick, but some gardeners don't know it. When you cut off your first head of broccoli leave the plant growing because numerous other little heads will develop. (See cabbage.)

CABBAGE (this suggestion includes broccoli, cauliflower, kale, brussels sprouts).—I plant seed in the open ground in May, but I don't like to transplant so I put sticks in the row eighteen inches apart and plant a few seeds by each stick. I thin it out gradually until I have one plant every eighteen inches. I let some of the extra plants get big enough to give away if I can find someone who wants them.

CARROTS.—These are slow to germinate and are always much too thick and rather hard to thin because they are so small. So I drop the seed in the drill and then drop radish seed on top of the carrot seed. This serves three purposes: radishes germinate quickly and mark the row; space is saved; when you pull the radishes you automatically thin the carrots somewhat. But not enough. I thin the carrots when they are big enough to eat, although still very tiny.

I make a second planting in early July; these never get large, but make tender little carrots to eat raw in October, November and December.

Many people don't know that you can leave carrots in the ground all winter. But if the ground freezes hard and then thaws, your carrots are likely to rot. At the first thaw you can dig them up and save them.

CAULIFLOWER.—Last summer John showed me a cute trick for bleaching cauliflower. The books tell you to tie the leaves together when the heads begin to form, but an effective and much quicker way is to break the leaves and let them lie over the head. Purple cauliflower, of course, does not need this treatment. (See cabbage for planting the seeds.)

CHINESE CABBAGE.—Good for greens, when you thin it.

CORN.—One thing the beginner should always remember is that corn simply refuses to germinate when the ground is dry. That which you plant in May and early June usually comes along splendidly, but I have at last got it into my head that corn planted in very dry weather has to be watered. Since one is watering only seeds, and not the roots of plants, one does not need very much.

I believe in growing vegetables in the smallest possible space to save work. Since I have been mulching, the soil will nourish things planted quite closely. I have been planting peas in rows three feet apart and then, when it is time to plant corn, I put that in, one and one-half feet from the rows of peas. When the pea vines are pulled out the corn is three feet apart with nothing in between.

However, I find that I must use plenty of mulch on both sides of the peas so they won't droop over the young corn. Also, I think it works out better if you don't grow peas on both sides of a row of corn. That is, put the peas six feet apart instead of three, and plant two rows of corn between the pea rows.

If you don't want to use arsenate of lead or crow repellent you can protect young corn as follows: take a suitable length of hardware cloth, sixteen to twenty-four inches wide, and bend at right angles at the center so that each side is from eight to twelve inches long. Hardware cloth is galvanized wire mesh. Use a mesh fine enough so that a crow can't get his bill through. Place these lengths firmly over a row of corn—like a long tent.

When the corn is two inches high you can remove the tent and transfer it to a row of younger corn.

I have worked out a satisfactory way of handling corn stalks. Of course I want to keep them right there in the garden for organic material and mulch, but they used to be cumbersome. Now when I go out to pick corn I take the clippers with me. When I gather the last ear from a stalk it takes only a few seconds to clip the stalk into pieces, say a foot long, and to pull up the root. Just let it lie there; by next spring it will be rotted or rotting nicely. Sometimes I can't pull the root out; I keep a thin, spadelike tool handy and dig up the root with it. John lets the roots stay in the ground; that may be better. By the time the last ear of corn is picked the problem of dealing with the stalks is behind you. Since I have been mulching I have never seen a corn borer, so the stalks do not contaminate the earth.

CUCUMBERS.—John gives me these by the bushel for pickling, so I put in only three or four hills. A simple time and space saving way to always have young ones is to plant the seeds two or three times, a few weeks apart, but in the same hills.

Since I have been mulching I no longer have to dig a hole and enrich the ground. Simply drop the seeds anywhere.

DANDELIONS.—They are not bitter when they are very young. If you pick them and put French dressing on them when they first show up in the spring you accomplish two things: get them out of the lawn, and have an early green on the table. But everyone knows that.

KOHLRABI.—Since I've been mulching I never thin them; the ground is rich enough to support them all. But they are so close together that if you pull one out you are likely to disturb the ones next to it. So I take a sharp knife and cut them off just below the bulb.

LETTUCE.—The earlier you get this in the better, you know that. In March Fred takes out my strawberry cold frames. I pull away the mulch from the spot I have chosen for lettuce and we put the cold frames over that spot. If the ground is still frozen it soon thaws. As soon as it is soft I put some cotton-seed meal along the row. Then I plant lettuce and put a row of beets in the same frame.

I thin lettuce after the plants get large enough to use. I could plant it the way I do the cabbage family—just as far apart as I want the heads to be—but I never have. It is surprising how rapidly it grows; we can never eat it fast enough to keep it thinned as much as the directions call for, although I begin picking it while it's tiny. However, my *Great Lakes,* six inches apart instead of the twelve to eighteen that the books insist on, gets huge.

ONIONS.—Be sure to harvest your large *Sweet Spanish* early enough. John thinks they don't keep well if you leave them out too long.

PARSLEY.—This germinates so slowly that I start it, too, under a portable cold frame. Sometimes I thin it and sometimes I don't; in a ten-foot row I have more than I can use, whichever I do, and I use a great deal of it.

Last fall, for the first time in many years, I made another attempt to grow parsley indoors all winter. I tried something new, but I didn't give it enough time, it didn't work, so I won't tell you about it!

When Rex saw it he told me this: Sometime in late June or early July take a large flowerpot and plant four parsley seeds in it and bury the pot in the garden. Pull out the weakest plant and keep this up until there is only one left. When the weather gets really cold take the pot indoors. He says he has fine parsley all winter that way. I am going to do it next year.

PEAS.—It is extremely helpful, both in picking and in keeping the pods from rotting in wet weather, to prop the vines up on both sides with plenty of mulch. I grow quite a lot of peas, but I never make a big job of picking them. I pick as long as I feel like it, mark where I left off and continue the next day.

PEPPERS.—Frost is sure to come along before the peppers all get red. I put my portable frames over them or toss some light mulch on them on a night which threatens to be cold. I could harvest them instead, but I like them all to get as red as possible. See *Spinach*.

PUMPKINS.—These and gourds and winter squash can drive you crazy. They ramble all over the garden; if you plant them among your corn you are always tramping on the vines. At last I think I've solved it. I'm going to put them all along the edge of the garden, just beyond the asparagus row—practically in the row—and let them wander where they are not a nuisance.

RADISHES.—I plant them in the same drills with carrots, parsley, and parsnips.

SPINACH.—Since this is harvested very early I put the pepper plants in the same row with it. It is wonderful raw, half and half with lettuce, some dill, parsley and French dressing.

SQUASH.—*Cocozelle* can be planted in a row of corn because it doesn't make a vine. See *Pumpkin* for winter squash.

TOMATOES.—I never stake them, let them run around over the mulch. One of the biggest problems here in the valley is to get tomatoes in early enough to have a long season. The trouble is they freeze so easily and we have had frost as late as June eighth.

I have finally got that problem solved, after twenty-five years of struggle, brainwork and heartache. I buy two well-advanced plants in pots, along with my regular plants. I put them in the ground about the middle of May and protect them as follows: If they are tall I plant them by laying them down and letting only the tops show above the ground. Then I put mulch around each plant, quite high, right up to the top leaves. Late in the afternoon, unless I am positive there will be no frost, I put a stiff plastic hotkap over each plant and over this a bushel basket. A really high wind could blow off both basket and hotkap, but with a high wind frost is unlikely. All you need do then is wander over the meadow and retrieve your hotkaps and baskets.

No plant has ever frozen with all that protection. It would be quite a performance if you had fifty plants or so, but I never grow more than two dozen nowadays, and once you get your hotkaps and baskets handy, it doesn't seem to me too high a price to pay for a long tomato season.

TURNIPS.—If you like the tops, thin them and eat them for greens.

If your garden is situated so that on one or more sides it adjoins grass or weeds you find that it is a constant fight to keep the latter from encroaching. If you cultivate the garden with a tractor you can cultivate a path all around it. But if you cultivate by hand, or if you mulch, you have to use some other method.

One way is to keep the mulch all around and right up against the garden. Another effective way is to make a path about a foot or two wide with magazines, thick layers of newspaper, or cardboard. I used to take cartons apart and make a nice neat path all around the garden, except on the side where witch grass was the near neighbor. There I had to dig a ditch. However, I got a letter from Scott a few days ago saying he is convinced that mulch will kill witch grass if you pile it on thickly enough. I think he means a mountain of it.

I find it handy to keep a bucket of lime and one of cottonseed meal sitting in the garden. I use garbage pails with tight-fitting lids for this.

Paint all handles of small garden tools a bright color. I can't tell you how much time I wasted looking for tools until John did that for me. Also, once in awhile I take a kitchen knife to the garden to cut off some kohlrabi, broccoli, and so on. I have formed a habit of always taking the same knife so that if I miss it I'll know where to look. If I miss another one I need not waste my time looking in the garden for it. Of course, this knife should be painted red, too; my little favorite is lying out there in the garden right now because I didn't get around to painting it.

When a sheet wears out, if you don't need it for other rags, tear it into broad strips for tying up the raspberries.

For raking back mulch when I am getting ready to plant

something, I like a light-weight, long-handled, four-pronged cultivator rather than a rake.

I never make a project of putting mulch on the garden. A few forksful every day or every other day doesn't cut into anything else you have to do and doesn't tire you.

Raking the leaves and getting them onto the garden is easy if you lay an old blanket on the ground, rake the leaves onto it, take the four corners and hold them together. Then either throw the blanket full of leaves over your shoulder or, if the leaves are wet and heavy, drag the blanket to the garden. Or put heavy leaves on something nearer—peonies. If the leaves are light enough to blow, throw a cauliflower root or some cornstalks on them.

If some member of the squash family shows up in the garden without my having planted it there I ruthlessly pull it out. One hates to, but once there were a few of them where I was going to plant the corn and I decided to leave them alone. Naturally, they got a head start and the poor little corn didn't have a chance. Also, naturally, they all turned out to be gourds, of which I didn't need so many, and the least attractive kind of gourds at that.

Scott says to plant the garden with the rows running north and south. This way the sun can get to the roots of things and most effectively do its share toward producing fine crops.

I no longer mark the rows with little sticks with names on them. It is easy to see what is where and I have a garden plan on paper if I should need it. When I plant two varieties of one vegetable, such as *America* and *Viking* spinach, I place them alphabetically so that I know which is which.

Everybody knows that the more things you can get done in the fall the better, for in spring there is so much to do. Sometimes I manage to get the corn rows all marked for next year and give them their allotment of cotton-seed meal. If you mark the rows with a stick they are likely to get knocked out or broken off. So at the beginning and end of each row I put a narrow board or strip of cardboard in place along the row and cover it with hay. It is pleasant, in May and June, just to fix your string and plant the corn and not have to take time marking the rows and putting cotton-seed meal down each row.

If you get tired squatting, kneeling and bending, you can sit. Mary uses a cushion. Fred made me a sturdy little wooden stool with a loop of cord attached so that I can hang it on my arm when I go to the garden with my hands full of other things. And Bob Allen gave me a kneeling stool with raised curved bars which you use to let yourself down and up. Also, there is a place in it for small tools. When I first saw it I thought it was a little la-de-da, but now I use it constantly and would hate to be without it.

In the spring, if the clumsy big things such as broccoli roots are still unrotted, as they get in your way toss them into the space allotted for tomatoes. Since you don't have to rake back the mulch to make a furrow for tomatoes, the coarser mulch won't interfere.

We all know we should take good care of our tools. Don't leave dirt on them; don't leave them out overnight. Put each one in its appointed place when you have finished with it for the day. This is a good rule and I believe in it most of the time. But on a day when I have worked a little too hard, a little too long, and the tool is in the garden and the tool shed is away down at the back of the barn, I ask myself: "Do I exist for my tools or do they exist for me?"

They are getting old and should be treated with decent consideration. But I am getting old, too; I also should be treated gently. So I lay the tool on the hay and lay myself on the couch and feel justified, but I do keep wondering if it is likely to rain before morning.

Man Shall Not Live by Bread Alone

WHEN I THINK BACK to my childhood the clearest picture I get of my mother is one where she is bending over a flower bed. She was still at it in her eighty-eighth year.

When my father died she came out early every spring with Mary and lived in the cottage which Charlie Stauffer had built for her. The neighboring farmers used to say to each other: "Spring is here. Mrs. Stout is digging around in a flower bed."

She hired a boy sometimes and Mary helped her a great deal; now and then she called on Fred or a barn guest for some job. She asked Jake Baker to do something for her one Sunday morning and he still enjoys telling about it.

Those were the days when great numbers of the intelligentsia began flocking to the country; the magazines and newspapers had jokes and cartoons about how hazardous it was to visit these eager folk, for you spent your week end slaving like a farm hand.

Jake had many of such friends and made it a point of honor not to lift a hand when he visited them. When they asked him to do something he would say that he was sorry, but he couldn't do it without a mattock and, since they didn't want to admit they didn't know what a mattock was, they would drop the subject. Jake would lie in the hammock while everyone else toiled.

When Mother asked him to dig up a small bridal-wreath bush which she wanted to transplant, Jake said as usual: "I'd love to, Mrs. Stout, but I'd have to have a mattock."

"You don't need a mattock," Mother said. "Here's a spade; if you don't know how to do it I'll show you."

Jake, who is an unusually versatile and knowledgeable person, knew very well how to do it; he transplanted the bush for Mother and enjoyed his defeat immensely.

The cottage was on a huge rock and Mother covered the top of it with myrtle, ivy, a particularly attractive variety of sedum, and pink lilies of the valley. Then down the side along with the vines she had mountain pink, grape hyacinths, violets, crocuses, and, at the bottom, a row of tulips.

She kept expanding and her entire yard gradually became a flower garden. Mary and I were a little desperate, trying to help her plant endless annuals. Early one spring Mary said to me: "Will you help Mother order her seeds and see if you can restrain her a little? I can't."

I went over to the cottage with pencil and paper and told Mother I would call off each flower and make out her order for her. I knew I couldn't talk her out of any particular flower and so I simply skipped a few of them.

Unfortunately, she knew the alphabet. I would say, for instance: "What about nasturtiums?"

"Oh, yes, we'll have to have—wait, that's *n.* What happened to balsam? Four o'clock—larkspur?"

So she planted everything, and when she ran out of space, flower beds began to show up in our lawn too. She loved to surprise us with them; what better thing could you possibly give a person than a new flower bed? When Fred and I went away for a few days for my birthday I knew perfectly well what we would come back to. And there it was: a new flower bed in front of the barn, planted with cosmos seed. The birthday bed.

One Sunday when my brother Walt and Walter Roddy, Virginia's father, were here, Mother suddenly had to have a large bed for Oriental poppies. It was the middle of summer and the books said to plant Oriental poppies in the autumn. Mother paid little attention to garden books; she would transplant any large plant, full of blossoms, on the hottest, driest day in July or August, water it plentifully and say to it firmly: "Now you grow." They always did; John insisted that they were afraid not to.

On this Sunday morning she put the two Walters to work spading up a big round flower bed not far from the birthday bed. If these two men were not lazy they loved to pretend to be, and with an appreciative audience of a dozen or so barn guests they put on quite an act.

The earth turned out to be nothing but gravel and stones, some of them immense. Finally it was ready to rake. They tied a garden rake in front of their car and finished the job, both sitting in the car, raking the bed by backing up. Virginia held up the rake for them each time they went forward.

It was, of course, a godsend to have someone making the place beautiful while I was so busy with vegetables. Mother loved doing it so much that no one had the heart to try to make her see reason. Fred said if we found we couldn't stop her any other way he would sell off all but one acre.

Whenever Mary and Mother took a drive over to see Rex, my eyes would meet Mary's, saying: "Do your best," and hers would answer: "You know perfectly well I'm helpless." She was, of course; they would come back loaded down with seeds, bulbs, roots, slips. Rex knew our problem, but how could he refuse her anything?

With Mary to keep house Mother spent every working minute in the garden. The only disaster she had was when she dug up some poison ivy in the woods and planted it all along the back of the woodshed. I don't think we could have had poison ivy in Kansas; she would have recognized it, if we had, and, too, I would have remembered if any of us had been poisoned by it.

Mother had a bad case of poisoning that time. Her comment was: "If only the bright men who run the world would busy themselves killing the poison ivy in it instead of killing each other we would all be better off."

I told her that William James had made a similar intelligent suggestion, but so far no one had paid any attention to it.

When Mother died in 1940 Mary and I took over the flowers

until Mary rented the cottage to a friend and spent most of her time in New York. The beds around the cottage had to go back to grass; no tenant would ever take over that much work.

Following is the limited list of the flowers I grow. I have omitted planting instructions which are easily available to everybody, but I have made some comments which may prove helpful.

Annuals

ALYSSUM.—I planted *Royal Carpet* alyssum for the first time last summer. I thinned some of it to six inches apart; some I didn't thin at all. Both made fine royal carpets. You can transplant it satisfactorily.

ASTERS.—I like to grow these, not only because they are lovely, but also because you have them in the fall when flowers are scarce. I prefer the single ones. I never had much luck with them until I read they should have partial shade and planted them on the east side of the kitchen. There they are in the shade all afternoon.

Since our season is so late I usually start asters in the cold frame, but last spring I put the seed in the open ground early in June. With the unusually cold summer we had, this meant that they did not begin to bloom until after Labor Day. They stayed fresh-looking and beautiful through several frosts, as they are not likely to do if they begin blooming earlier.

CALIFORNIA POPPY —It would seem a pity not to grow this charming little yellow flower. It seeds itself and is in almost constant bloom from May until mid-October. But look under *Tulips* to see what I have done with it.

LOBELIA.—Mother got Mary and me started on this appealing little flower. Each spring she would buy a few plants from a greenhouse and put them around here and there in her garden. When I began to plan the few remaining flower beds, I wanted a border of lobelia around one of them, but it was too expensive to buy enough plants for a border. The seeds germinate so slowly that they have to be started indoors in February or March. I tried it, but didn't have any luck.

Finally, I asked Mr. Mead, from whom I bought my tomato plants, to start lobelia seeds for me. Then he could sell me a whole flat of tjny plants and I would not have to pay the price of large individual plants. He did this and the result is a bed of flowers so gay and lovely that it is quite beyond describing. I will tell more about it under *phlox drummondi.*

MORNING-GLORY.—In Kansas these were weeds which had to be hoed out of the corn constantly, but that didn't prejudice me against them. I stick to *Heavenly Blue;* last year I bought a packet of *Scarlet O'Hara,* but Fred thought it would be a pity to change the effect of the great curtain of blue behind the roses so I gave the red ones away.

·PETUNIAS.—Plant petunias just once—then try to get rid of them. We grew them for several years; then we wanted the space for other things and pulled them up when they appeared. Along came a year so dry the lawn got as brown as a dead leaf and even peonies, rose bushes and lilacs began to droop. Every annual died except the petunias. Right there in the valley of death they were the only green thing there was, living gallantly on, making spots of color. I felt humbled by their generosity after the way I had treated them.

I didn't go back later to giving them a place of their own; I wasn't that remorseful. But I do leave many of them alone; they show up among the portulaca, asters, zinnias. The only place where they are not allowed at all is the sacred lobelia and *phlox drummondi* bed. They even smile at me from behind a cabbage or a carrot now and then in the vegetable garden.

PHLOX DRUMMONDI.—For these I use the large circular bed which the two Walters raked with their automobile. The entire center is filled with dwarf annual phlox which has every color there is, I think, except the yellow shades. The border is dark-blue lobelia.

Because of the short season I usually start the phlox in the cold frame. It is a lot of work to transplant them for there are so many and they are so small. I cover each plant with a raspberry box and John has named that bed Levittown.

Last spring I planted the seed in the bed in rows six inches apart. We had an unusually cold June; the germination was sparse and slow and I had just barely enough plants to fill the bed. In fact, I put a few left-over lobelia in some empty spots. Planting this way meant that the bed was late in flowering, but it also meant that it was still perfectly lovely all through September and part of October. Next spring I am going to plant them the same way, but I am also going to put some seeds in the cold frame, for spares. This will give me more than enough to fill the bed.

I plant the lobelia more closely than the book says, so that it will make a heavy border. In dry weather it must be watered or it will give up. This is my favorite bed and is the only one I water. In dry weather, when I might get frowned at if I used the precious well water for a flower bed, I keep the big watering pot by the kitchen sink. Into this goes all the water I use for washing vegetables, rinsing dishes and so on. This way I am obliged to water the lobelia and *phlox drummondi* piecemeal, but I keep them watered. They are worth any amount of trouble. And, of course, they don't need nearly as much watering as they would if I didn't mulch them.

That bed is both brilliant and sensational, but, at the same time, so dainty that nobody could possibly call it brash.

PORTULACA.—I prefer the old-fashioned name for this: rose moss. Twenty-five years ago Mother sowed some seed in a triangular bed just beyond the east kitchen window. In each corner of the triangle she planted a rosebush. The bed is still there. It seeds itself each year; all the care it needs is thinning. When it is at its best you could almost call it amusing. The only thing I have against it is that it is too temperamental. It opens and closes erratically. The only thing you can depend on is that it will close up when someone is coming who would particularly like to see it.

SWEET PEAS.—I believe that these are difficult to grow in Connecticut—most of the people around here say they have no luck. Few people in our locality even try. I have grown them every year for twenty-five years, that is, I have put in the seed and some plants came up. I can't truthfully say that I have picked blossoms every year.

Mother and I both tried hard; it was one of the few flowers I worked at while she was alive. We followed all the rules. We were told to dig a deep trench and fill it with rotted manure mixed with earth and we did it. We watered the plants religiously. Sometimes we had fair luck, usually we had none. We put some over by the cottage, some near the barn, some in the vegetable garden, eager to please them.

Then I began to mulch. I stopped digging a trench, simply planted the seeds in the vegetable garden in a furrow three inches deep, stopped watering them, and, for the past eight years or longer, I have had quantities of beautiful sweet peas right up to early September. I feel very sad that I couldn't have learned that earlier, while Mother was alive to enjoy it.

VERBENAS.—Next to lobelia and *phlox drummondi* I think the verbena bed is the loveliest. It has the same habit of taking one's breath away.

In my experience the seeds germinate rather sparsely and slowly, but a packet of seed will give you plenty for a good-sized bed because the plants sort of creep and spread. If you plant them a foot apart they will cover the entire bed.

I had always planted these in the cold frame until this year. (I have been saying that about all the flowers; the truth is that lettuce, spinach and radishes were having a spring festival in the cold frame and there was no room for flower seeds. I won't do that again.)

Of course, I *would* try putting verbenas in the open ground during an unusually cold spring. They need to be quite warm for germinating, and the result was that only one plant came through. However, that one plant, uncrowded as it was, almost filled the bed. It was amazing.

ZINNIAS.—See Tulips, below, under "Bulbs."

Perennials

CHRYSANTHEMUMS.—I have only one relatively early blooming variety of white ones which a neighbor gave me. I love chrysanthemums, but there is no use trying to have them in a place like ours, where the cold weather comes so early.

FORSYTHIA.—This sends out roots which can be transplanted; I've given away dozens of them. Don't buy any; ask some friend to hunt around under his bush and find you a root. Here in the cold valley our forsythia bush has bloomed only four times in twenty-four years. I used to think that something was wrong with the bush; now I think it must be the valley.

LILAC.—This is, of course, past master at making new bushes. At a rough guess I could give you at least five hundred lilac bushes right now if you wanted to dig them up.

LILY OF THE VALLEY.—Fred, my sister Juanita, and her husband dug up some roots in an abandoned cemetery down the road the first year we came here. They planted them on the north side of the house. The bed gave up some years later, but in the meantime Mother had made another bed around an old apple tree and that is still in good health. I mail a few hundred sprays each spring to friends in New York. There is a bed of pink ones at the cottage.

Last spring Bob Allen gave me a lily-of-the-valley tree. It is supposed to be covered with real honest-to-goodness lilies of the valley. Now it is only a foot high. I may not live to see it bloom, but I hope someone will.

MOUNTAIN PINK.—This is tremendously satisfactory. Mother put some in her rock garden about twenty years ago. I would guess that she planted a dozen roots, and all of the mountain pink we have now came from those. Also, I have given away many roots.

In the front of our house around the mailbox is a large triangular spot which was ugly for years. Mother struggled with it, trying one thing after another, but the earth is almost entirely gravel and nothing lived. Once Rex sent his gardener over with a station wagon full of something or other to plant there for Mother. Then came a dry spell, we couldn't water it, and it died.

Finally, after I began to mulch and had time to spare, I tackled that triangle. I dug up some mountain pink from the cottage and put it there. It spread. I dug up more and also separated that which I had planted. It has taken me, and it, eight years to cover the entire spot, but at last there is a solid mass of white and pink there. Because it is so large it is quite striking when in bloom. No car passes without stopping and people make special trips to look at it and take color pictures.

I like it and I am glad it is there, but it is not nearly as beautiful as the verbena and *phlox drummondi* beds are. It is the size that makes it impressive. I did it for only one reason, because Mother worked so hard to do something about the ugliness of that spot. It is a memorial to her. I am telling you about it because there is no question of this: mountain pink is an excellent ground cover and will thrive in the most miserable soil.

ORIENTAL POPPY.—This large, brilliant flower is certainly attractive, and blooms early when you are hungry for some color, but it has never learned to cooperate very well. If the weather doesn't suit it perfectly it misbehaves. Also, it blooms for a short time and then is ugly for quite awhile. Mother put it in the big automobile-raked bed, but she soon saw that was a mistake, and we moved them up against the barn where they make a fine dash of color in the spring but are not conspicuous during their unattractive period. They multiply rapidly; you always have some roots to give away.

PEONIES.—We have a great many of these. Twenty years ago Rex gave me enough to make a hedge all around the lily and frog pond which Fred dug to the left of the rose-moss bed. Hal Hirsch helped me put them in; neither one of us knew quite what we were doing, but they came out all right. We also have them under the kitchen window and a row along the end of the drive near the barn. By far the loveliest ones are those Rex gave Mother—huge single ones, white, pink, and red. The white ones look fragile and ethereal, fairy-like. But they wear well; I have mailed buds to New York and they carry splendidly.

I was told that peonies were gross feeders so I gave them all plenty of manure. But for the last ten years I have given them nothing at all except their own tops when they die, and fallen leaves. Some of ours are in full sun, some are under trees; they seem to do equally well.

I de-bud some of them; others I leave alone and let all the buds make blossoms. This way I have both size and quantity.

I don't take the tops off until spring. I have seen peony beds cleaned up in early fall, with the tops cut off and carried away and the ground around the peonies bare and neat. Even before I began to mulch everything this seemed wrong and positively cruel to me, the poor things looked so cold and miserable.

PHLOX.—Mother put in some perennial phlox years ago and it behaves somewhat the way petunias do: pops up all over the place. The color becomes pale and uninteresting if you don't keep them picked, but when the flowers show up in areas which would otherwise be a tangle of weeds we are grateful for them. I no longer have any that I take care of.

ROSES.—There have been whole books written on roses, but I could put on one page all I know about them. It will be more to the point to tell you what I do not do for them than what I do.

Since I've been mulching them, theoretically I have stopped spraying, but about once a season John spots some aphids on them and either hounds me into giving them some nicotine or, if I'm stubborn, does it himself. As for black leaf spot, everyone I know who grows roses sprays for that and yet has it as badly as, or worse than, I do. So I do nothing.

For many years the only food the roses have had is mulch and they perform satisfactorily compared with those I have had opportunities to see. I know they should have more water than they get and I would be glad to oblige, but when they are short of water, so is our well, and I have no choice.

In the winter, as you probably know, you are supposed to pile dirt high around your roses. Don't use leaves; everyone tells you that these make a cozy nest for mice and the mice will chew your roses. I get the dirt from between my two rows of asparagus, where mulch has been rotting for years. This is as good as manure. Then when spring comes I spread it out and around the rosebushes.

It would be as unsuitable for me to tell you what variety of rose to buy as to choose your dress or necktie for you. But I do want to tell you about *Radiance*.

It is an undistinguished rose, an everyday pink in color, with nothing special about size or form. I'll tell you what it's like: the chair in your room which no one would pick out as handsome but which, among your fine pieces of furniture, is certainly not offensive. The springs never break, the upholstery doesn't show the dirt or wear out, it never creaks under the heaviest occupant, the rungs never get loose, and it is comfortable to sit in.

Mother planted our *Radiance* in the far corner of the rose-moss bed twenty-five years ago. It is the only hybrid tea rose I have which does not have black leaf spot. It has never had an off year. It is the first to bloom and the last to stop blooming. It has many times as many flowers as any other kind we have.

The blossoms are neither extra large nor extra small. The fragrance cannot compete with some of the white varieties, but it smells like a rose. The bush is large and sturdy. It is by far the most dependable hybrid tea I know about. With all of these outstanding virtues I am almost ashamed to say that it is not my favorite. If I have a favorite, perhaps it is *Countess Vandal*.

Climbing roses don't suffer from black leaf spot (at least mine don't) and neither does our charming, early-blooming *Rose Hugonis*. This latter sometimes makes a separate root near the mother bush which you can take up and transplant.

I have been told that when you pick a rose you should cut it just above a five-leaf formation rather than a three-leaf one.

Bulbs

CROCUSES.—I don't understand these. John is a better, more scientific gardener by far than I am, but crocuses won't do much of anything for him. While for me they not only multiply surprisingly, but, like petunias, they jump around all over the place. I stuck one white bulb and one purple one in the rose-moss bed some years ago and now there is a great clump of each in spite of the fact that I tell John every year to dig up some more for himself. The whole bed is spotted with them although I planted only two bulbs. I planted a row of them all around the peony hedge, which multiplies rapidly.

Have you noticed that the yellow crocuses are always the first to bloom and also that yellow seems to be the early color? Forsythia and daffodils are both yellow and they are about the first things you see in the garden after the crocuses.

DAFFODILS.—I put one bulb in the center of the rose-moss bed about eight years ago and this spring I counted ninety-three blossoms. They are extremely large, with very long stems, but they are just the everyday variety. There is a great long row of daffodils and narcissus at the cottage which have been there for twenty years or more. I have given away hundreds of bulbs and still there are many hundreds of blossoms every year.

GRAPE HYACINTHS.—I have been talking in hundreds; now we'll skip to thousands. I have these also around the peony hedge and I know I have given away at least ten thousand bulbs, probably more. I accomplished this by digging up a great clump of them every time anyone shows up who has a spot of ground somewhere, wrapping them in a piece of paper, and thrusting them on the victim while I talk rapidly about something else, so my caller won't notice what's going on. Nobody wants a few hundred bulbs, but I have to do something with the surplus.

TULIPS.—We have a row of these from the house out to the *phlox drummondi* bed. In Chapter Fourteen I make some rude remarks about experts and their attitude to tulips, so I won't go into that here.

Tulips are ugly when they are through blooming since you are obliged to let the tops die right where they are. You must let them alone until they come out easily with a gentle pull. Ours are in a conspicuous place and something has to be done to take the curse off the dying tops.

Many years ago Mother planted California poppy seed all along the tulip row. They seed themselves, are quite charming, and give us a mass of yellow blossoms almost as soon as the tulips stop blooming. If you keep the seed pods picked off you will get blossoms until after the first frosts. They are never quite so profuse later as they are in the spring when you need them most on account of the tulip tops, but there are always a few. Except for thinning in the early spring, this picking off of the seed pods is the only work connected with California poppies, and it is a little tedious. I am lucky; my sisters, Elizabeth and Mary, are here a good deal in the summer and they, and other barn guests, seem rather to like the job.

In this same row I always plant zinnias. Fred likes them for their color; Mary doesn't care much for them, she says they look uncomfortable. She is right; they are stiff. The new cactus-flowered zinnias which I got last summer seem a little less tense than the others.

The tulip row is gay from very early spring to frost.

*   *   *

And now for our barberry hedge—but this is an obituary and still a slightly delicate topic in our household.

The second or third year we were here we planted a row of

them all along the driveway. Rex suggested it; it was the only really bad thing he ever did to me except once, when we were youngsters, and he persuaded Dad that it was his turn to read *The Youth's Companion* first when it was absolutely my turn.

The hedge grew rapidly and was attractive, especially in fall and winter when it was covered with red berries. We began to notice that everywhere we went around the place we ran into a barberry bush. They became somewhat of a nuisance.

Through the years I raked the leaves off the lawn and took them to the garden. Before I would get around to it the bulk of them would blow as far as the barberry hedge and lodge there. I could have left a few, but such heaps of them looked ugly; besides I wanted to use the leaves. The bad feature was that I got thorns mixed in with the leaves and was constantly going to Fred to get a thorn taken out of my fingers.

I hate thorns, and more or less unconsciously I must have grown to hate the barberry hedge. For when John said to me, two years ago: "If you would take out those damned barberry bushes you could put your *Rose Hugonis* right here," I said, "Wonderful! Would you have time to take them out?"

I knew he hated them and now he said fervently: "It would be such a pleasure I wouldn't even let you pay me for the job."

I consulted Fred; he was against it because he liked the looks of the hedge and his birds liked the seeds. Comes the day when we are so poor that Fred has to choose which one to feed, me or the birds, I know, unfortunately, who will go hungry.

I had visions now of a life without barberries and I brought forth every argument I could think up. The one that did the trick for me was that, someday, I would be an old, tired woman and wouldn't be able to face the mean, thorny job of cleaning up under those bushes every fall. Fred hadn't known at all what a pain that job was; now he gave in and went back into the house.

The bushes were huge; John had to tie them to his car and pull them out that way. When he had got three of them out he said: "Well, that's it."

"Can you do the rest tomorrow?" I asked him.

"What rest?"

"The rest of the row."

He looked at me in amazement.

"Do you mean you are going to take them all out?"

"Sure."

"Won't Fred have a stroke?"

I told him that Fred had agreed. John had heard only a part of our conversation and thought I was mistaken; he worked far past his lunchtime to get them all out before Fred would see what was going on and stop him.

I was not mistaken; Fred had really given in, but he still heaves a regretful sigh now and then. I think down in his heart (and someday he may admit it) he agrees that the row of roses and holly which he and John put along the driveway last fall is much lovelier. And we get a view across the meadow now which we didn't have before.

Last autumn, after twenty-five years of playing the role of audience as far as flowers went, Fred took a sudden, not to say violent, interest in landscaping. He grabs the pickaxe and begins digging up stuff—anything that lies in his path. It makes me mildly nervous, wondering which of my prizes will come up next.

Of course, I am exaggerating; he will be careful of my pets. He is confining his activities more or less to the frog pond, which has always been his domain in a way, although up to now he let it take care of itself. Mother used to call it "Fred's playpen."

For me, the rather embarrassing thing about Fred's activities will be that when he has finished it, the playpen will be the second most attractive thing in the whole yard. The first is the large, shallow birdbath in the lawn, surrounded with various kinds of sedum and a little evergreen tree at one end. Who laid it out? Fred, of course.

Mulching flowers

The most difficult thing to convince people about mulch is that it does not have to be ugly. Nor expensive; you don't have to buy peat moss. I don't buy anything; my one expense is to pay someone to bring Art's spoiled hay to me. Art wants to save me even that expense. He says if I will pay to have it baled, fifteen cents a bale, he will bring it down piecemeal in his milk truck.

Peat moss is fine, if you can afford it. Betty and Herbert Symonds do a beautiful job with it on their flower beds.

Bushes, such as peonies, may be mulched with their own tops and dead leaves without, I think, offending the eye. They grow so fast and get large so soon that the period of having to look at what surrounds them is very short.

Roses need a better looking mulch. This can be achieved by using a good thick layer of well-rotted hay and on that putting a thin layer of top earth from your vegetable garden. This cannot sprout weed seeds because of the thick layer of mulch underneath.

A few weeks ago I got another idea. Through the winter I am saving the coffee grounds, drying them, mixing them with a little wood ashes to get the color of earth. I do this on the large workbench in the kitchen which Fred built for me, and when people come in I point to it and ask: "What is that?" They all think it is dirt.

In the spring I'll put this on top of the rose mulch. I defy it to grow a weed, and it will look like dirt. One more good reason for drinking real coffee instead of instant.

A cross between the peony and rose methods can be used around things as large as zinnias, marigolds, etc. The mulch here need not be quite as neat as that around roses but somewhat neater than peony mulch. Once you start you will work out your own system.

The mulch around smaller things—verbenas, *phlox drummondi*, etc.—must be much finer than any of the others, both because the coarse mulch would be too difficult to handle here, and for looks. I get this from the vegetable garden. There is always a great deal of material there which is just about through with being mulch, about ready to be called rich dirt. It is still coarse enough to discourage weed seeds from trying to sprout in it. I take a few wheelbarrowsful of this and spread it thickly around all small plants—plants, that is, which never will be large and bushy. It looks like earth, keeps weeds down, and keeps the ground soft and moist. And rots still more and becomes rich soil.

Mulching a bed which seeds itself, such as rose moss and California poppies, takes a little special treatment. I leave a thick mulch on these beds all winter. In the spring I take off the heaviest part of the mulch and toss it under the peonies. Both California poppies and rose moss come up much too thickly for their own good (perhaps that is true of most things that seed themselves—petunias, certainly, and dill) and therefore if a considerable number of the seeds are frustrated by mulch, that is all to the good.

To someone who has not used this system I should think it might sound like a lot of work. It is work, but it takes not one tenth and perhaps not one fiftieth of the time consumed in keeping weeds out of the beds all summer and going through some other performance—manure, fertilizer—to enrich the soil.

Speaking of fertilizer, my roses have never even heard of anything such as vigoro, and the like, and would wonder what on earth was going on if I began digging around their roots, giving them this peculiar stuff to eat. I have a definite feeling that they wouldn't like it.

Have I any flower tricks you may not have thought of? Here is one my sister Juanita taught me: If you have a plant, or row of plants, which flop over and you don't want to stake them, take wire coat hangers, straighten out the hook part so that you can stick it into the ground near the plant, pull the other part into a triangle, and you have an adequate and inconspicuous support. I used to do this all along the row of peas until I took to mulching and piling hay against them.

I feel about landscaping as I do about interior decorating: even if you know you have no creative artistic ability it is more interesting and more enjoyable to arrange, yourself, the house

you are going to live in, the yard you are going to look at, than
to hire someone to do it for you. It is one thing to walk through
a museum and admire what others have done; it is something
else to look at a bed of flowers and say to yourself: "I never
should have put those two things in the same bed. Next year,
I'll try—" Or to say: "Did *I* really think that up? It is so
lovely!"

Few of us can paint a picture and have it hung in a museum.
Many of us can experiment with flowers, and all of us can give
some thought to beautifying the house or furnished room we
live in.

Anyone can figure out that he has to put a tall plant behind
a low-growing one if he wants to see both. Take it from there.

You may not know what color "goes" with what other color,
but surely you know which ones you like to see together. Is
your garden for you or for visitors? All of your friends haven't
the same taste and preferences; you cannot possibly cater to
them all. So cater to yourself.

I was a little insincere awhile ago when I said that Fred's
birdbath was the most attractive thing in the yard. I think the
phlox drummondi bed is and possibly that is because I planned
it myself.

I believe that it is important for a person's home and clothes
and yard to express his own personality and not the taste of
some outsider. To me, hiring an interior decorator or landscape
gardener is a little like learning fine sentences out of a book
and using them when you talk. They may be much more elegant
than any you could have thought up, but they are not you.

Planning a garden is like planning a way of life; arrange it
to please yourself, copying neither convention, nor tradition,
nor any individual, enjoy it and hope that a few other people
besides you will be pleased with it.

Am I preaching? Surely a chapter on flowers is no place for
a sermon. If anything in this world attends to its own little
affairs, doing the best it can with what it has to work with, and
never a word to anyone else of criticism or advice, it is a flower.

When the Days Begin to Lengthen

"WHEN THE DAYS BEGIN TO LENGTHEN, then the cold begins to strengthen." They begin to lengthen on the first day of winter, which surprised me when I first realized it. One hears so much of the long evenings of winter that one is likely to overlook the fact that autumn has exactly the same number.

Spring is my favorite season and I have always loved both summer and autumn. Formerly I didn't care much for winter, but here in the country I have grown to love it too. There is a privacy about it which no other season gives you. If you belong to yourself in the sense in which I think Montaigne meant it when he said the greatest thing in the world is to learn to belong to yourself, no one can take that gift away from you. And yet in spring, summer and fall people sort of have an open season on each other; only in the winter, in the country, can you have longer, quieter stretches when you can *savor* belonging to yourself.

I like the feeling of getting completely away from the garden when the cold weather sets in. Fred would like to surprise me some October morning after the first hard frost with a cozy little hothouse for me to play in all winter. He can't quite believe me when I assure him I don't want one.

I truly don't. Growing things is like every other pleasure I have heard of: one enjoys it more keenly if one takes a rest from it.

The number of weeks in a year in which all jobs are unrelated to the garden are few. Until the ground is frozen fairly hard there is something to do. Raking leaves and spreading them and other mulch over the garden is pleasant exercise in October. Pruning and tying up the raspberries, digging up rhubarb roots to give away, putting hay on the strawberries, hauling rich dirt for the rosebushes, pulling up the frozen flowers, mulching flower beds—all of these are October and early November jobs.

When the ground freezes seriously and seems inclined to stay frozen, if there is no deep snow I take my little hand axe and cut down some minor trees for next year's pole beans. I suppose I should not have to do this each year, but selecting and putting in poles is not my most outstanding talent and my poles are lucky if they don't have to give up the first year before the beans are all picked.

Just this minute it occurred to me that my sewing trick might be useful here. I can't sew. I can get a button on and I can get a hole in a sock pulled together somehow and that's it. Years ago I formed the habit of getting out some mending when a good seamstress was here for the week end. I would thread a needle and start the job. No seamstress could possibly stand watching me trying to mend. If I would start putting in the bean poles when some man was around I am sure I would get the same good results.

I choose a bright day to tidy up and clean the tool shed. The sun shines in the open door and keeps me warm. I like a sunny day, too, for taking the ashes out of the fireplace and sifting them over the wheelbarrow in the shed. I do this only two or three times a winter, for we like a good-sized pile of ashes to build a fire on.

When we had our stone fireplace built the mason made a hole in the bottom of it which you can uncover, then push the ashes through to the cellar. A wonderful masculine invention! Instead of sitting on a stool in front of the fireplace and comfortably taking out the ashes, you push them into the cellar, then go down there and, without a stool and without comfort, shovel them into a bucket and drag them back upstairs.

I ignore that fine invention. No doubt it was intended to save getting the room dirty, but women have brains, too. All you need to do is take out the ashes just before you vacuum. Since you go over the whole room anyway, what do you care if the vacuum cleaner has a little extra dust to pick up?

Fred shovels the snow unless I am in a mood to help. I love the job when conditions are perfect: early morning, snow dry and light, a brilliant sun, no wind, and I feeling vigorous. Otherwise I let Fred do it.

When the really cold weather sets in I take a rest from the garden and even stop thinking about it. But I want some outdoor exercise, and walking without a destination doesn't appeal to me. If there is not much snow around Christmas time I like to go to the woods and look for ground pine. All through the coldest months, if snow doesn't prevent, I like to pick up fallen branches and, with my small hand axe, chop some wood.

The various men around have said some pretty impudent things about my woodchopping. For instance, I carried in a really man-sized log one day and John asked: "What are you going to do with that?"

Offguard, I answered him: "Burn it, of course."

He said: "Don't you think it's done enough for you? It's already kept you warm for a couple of weeks while you chopped it."

And Fred says it is too confusing to try to build a fire with my contributions—he can't tell the logs from the matches.

Earlier in the season than one might think, since I honestly like a vacation from the garden, I begin to look forward to March. In January the seed catalogs begin to show up and I get on the couch before a fire built with my personally chopped logs and order my seeds.

Flowers take longer than vegetables. If only they wouldn't have those lovely colored pictures it would not be such a strain on my will power. But I am fairly well supplied with self-discipline and, however strong the pull, I won't permit myself to order more than enough seeds to fill the existing flower beds.

I send off the order and, some days later, the seeds arrive, and that gives me another pleasant task: arranging the packets alphabetically in three cigar boxes marked "Early," "Middle," "Late."

This happens in January. Later, when I find myself glancing at the calendar rather often, I stretch out on the couch again, this time with a large sheet of white paper, pen and ruler.

Now I plan next year's garden, and if you do not already know it you would be surprised to find how much time this saves you in the planting season and how many mistakes you avoid. I could do this once for all, I suppose, but I usually make a few changes—add a vegetable, plant more or less of another one than I had last year. Besides, why do myself out of the fun of drawing a new diagram every year? It's an ideal January occupation.

This is the time of year when your dinner guests can help choose the menu. In May and June there is little choice; they get spinach, asparagus, lettuce. Next, peas and collards, then string beans.

But in the winter, when we are having cocktails with our guests I ask them what are their favorite vegetables, and that is what they get.

I don't go in for many house plants. When Mother was alive she filled the cottage with them in the fall and when she went to New York in December we would move them all over to our place. She couldn't bear to have a plant die and you would hardly believe the great number of things Mary and I would dig up out of Mother's garden, put into pots, and drag into the house. The most nightmarish of all were huge marigolds, which I've never cared for much even when they stayed out of doors where they belong.

We had difficulty finding enough tables and benches to put everything on. Two of Fred's tables got ruined, a small painted one and a larger, much better one, but Fred loved Mother so much I think she could have spoiled all of his furniture without his saying a word.

We could have thrown everything out as soon as Mother set off for New York since she never came out in the winter and since most of the things were not expected to last very long, but somehow we never did. I suppose it would have seemed to us that we were betraying a trust; also, I didn't like to be the cause of a plant dying, even a marigold. So they were all allowed to live their allotted time. I don't think I even cheated a little by forgetting to water them.

I do have a few house plants now, things that have been given to me. There's a cheerful, funny little oxalis hanging in the kitchen window, in constant bloom all winter long. I recommend it highly.

I have a hoya leaf which is, I believe, from South America and is supposed to be something quite startling. I had that thing standing there in a little pot for nearly two years, waiting for something to happen. Nothing ever did. It made me think of a child who has been put in his room for punishment and is not allowed to come out until he says he is sorry. He won't give in, just sits and sulks. That little leaf just sat there for two years and it seemed to me that it was sulking.

Then one evening Rex was here and was amazed when I told him how long little hoya had been static, amazed when I told him I had never dug it up to see what was going on, if anything.

"I never dig things up," I said. He looked disappointed, and I added: "But I'm not against other people doing it."

Eagerly he took it out of its pot and we found healthy little roots. He put it back in the pot with some fresh rich dirt. That was about two months ago. Again it is just sitting there, but I have the feeling that it is no longer sulking.

Do you know Patience? Someone gave me a small plant, and if you feel, as I did, that you can't grow anything as other people seem to be able to do, by cutting off a slip and putting it in water, get yourself a Patience and give your ego a treat. I have grown dozens of these little plants to give away.

The first winter my tiny Patience grew so tall that I had

to prop it against the window. I was quite proud of myself. Isn't it interesting how easy it is for us to convince ourselves that we are clever? I never did a thing for that plant except to water it and yet, whenever I looked at it blooming merrily and getting bigger by the minute, I would think: Just see what I did!

That makes me think of what Fred said once when we were driving in New York through particularly difficult traffic. He began to laugh; I asked him what was funny, and he said: "I was thinking how skillful I am, handling my car in such traffic, and then I realized that all the other drivers are doing all right too."

I put Patience out of doors in the spring. Then I saw that my great achievement had a drawback. The thing was so big it couldn't stand up, and I had to cut it down to almost nothing.

After three years I got awfully bored with Patience. I put it out of doors one spring, pretending to myself that it was not too early, that it wouldn't freeze. It did, and I was careful not to mention it for fear someone would start me another.

Our philodendron is a little miracle. Mother had it in the cottage and, when Mary rented the cottage to the Kallgrens, Bethany said she would like to have it. She took care of it for three years and then she moved and the cottage was vacant for the winter months. In early spring Mary came out and, to my horror, found that the philodendron had been forgotten. I had intended taking it to our house and it had slipped my mind. It didn't look quite dead and I told Mary I would try to revive it.

It was a year before it decided to forgive me and resurrect itself. Then it began to grow again and we let it climb up the southwest window. It has now crept all along the ceiling on the west end of the room and is halfway along the north wall, heading east. I wish Mother could see it.

What did I do to revive it? Nothing much. I kept it watered and gave it a bit of manure, which is the only thing I have ever done for any house plant except to give them their own leaves as they fall off, if the plant is healthy.

I have something which Bess Conescu says is jade; it looks a little like a tortured cactus. Fred likes it. And I have a white rose begonia which outgrows its pots so fast I can hardly keep it supplied with bigger ones.

Four African violets—pink, white, light blue, dark blue. Bob Allen gave me Blue Girl; it was sort of miserable looking and I put it in a bigger pot. The leaves got so large that every time Betsy and Bob came to see us they gazed at Blue Girl with admiration and wonder. (The admiration was for me.) How it bloomed!

In quick succession I was given the other three violets and I put them all in big pots. They all stayed in constant luxuriant blossom; I was proud of myself and told all my friends that there was nothing to growing African violets—simply put them in big pots.

Then they stopped blooming, all of them, and didn't start again. That went on all through the summer, fall and winter. Last spring I was so annoyed with them that, having read that you must never put them out of doors, I promptly set them all in the yard, to live or die as they saw fit.

They began to bloom.

Now they are back in the house again, doing exactly as they please, which is very little. Betsy and Bob were here the other evening and Bob said they needed more light. I told him they had had that very same light during their blooming years. Even Bob doesn't know everything about African violets.

The experts know all about them, the catch being that the experts differ. One of the first things I read was that water on the leaves would turn them brown. I didn't believe it, but I asked Fred to water them; I hated to be the one to ruin them. Fred got the leaves good and wet and, of course, nothing happened. In the sun, out of the sun, lots of water, little water—people don't agree about African violets.

My carefully-thought-out opinion is that they are individuals and have a lot of character and do as they please. Also, I think they are like crows—that is, they have a sense of humor and get a kick out of going along with you on your pet theory just long enough to tempt you to make a fool of yourself by holding forth about how smart you are, and then they go into their shell and leave you looking silly. They love that; mine are irritated with me now because I'm on to them. That's why they've gone on strike.

I have one house plant which is such a sensation that it steals the show completely, not even minding that there is not much of a show to steal. In 1939 John gave Mother and me each a tiny gardenia from a cutting of a plant which belonged to Mrs. Maiga, a friend of his who is a genius with flowers. When Mother died a year later Mary gave her plant to Rex.

Mine did pretty well for a few years and then it seemed to go backward. This was during the period when John was away, so I couldn't ask his advice. I became discouraged with it and one day, when we were at the Krutch's for dinner and I realized again how good Joe was with house plants, I gave it to him. It picked up amazingly. After a year or two he generously offered to give it back to me, but I was too much of a lady to accept it.

John came back and, when he heard my sad tale, he gave me his gardenia, which was the same age as mine, but larger. It was a tremendous plant by then and his excuse for being so generous was that it was too big for his house, which, as a matter of fact, was true. Then Joe and Marcelle moved to Arizona and Joe gave his gardenia to Virginia.

I am going to have more to say about the care of gardenias in the next chapter, but since it is the only house plant I am thoroughly proud of, I didn't want to leave it out of my otherwise uninspiring report of potted plants.

As you are just about settling down to a long, hard winter with snow, slippery roads, chances of an ice storm and electricity going off, here comes February. The days are getting noticeably longer, there is a morning now and then which is almost like spring, and everybody is calling up everybody to report the first robin or redwing. You step out of doors and see a chipmunk; the sun is hot, not merely warm, and however cold it may be later, today you can go out without a coat. On a morning like this you are well disciplined indeed if you can resist going to the cold frame, getting out the sash, and starting rows of lettuce, radishes, spinach.

Then comes March, which was always my least favorite month in New York, with its violent and impertinent winds, its bitter cold days, more disagreeable than midwinter, no matter what the thermometer said.

March in the country is quite different. Cold and windy, to be sure, a good deal of the time, but the exciting things that happen in this otherwise unattractive month make up for any amount of discomfort.

Glory of the Snow, crocuses, serene, bright, and brave, daffodils and grape hyacinths pushing through the mulch, even tulips showing up toward the end of the month. Keep them covered a little longer; there will be many a frost still, hard enough to kill them if they are allowed to hurry.

Lilac buds are swelling; grass and chives begin to remind us that they were green once and soon will be again. Squirrels seem friskier; redwings waken you in the morning. Now dandelions are offering you either a problem or a meal, whichever way you choose to take them. They are quite pretty, you know; why don't you eat what you can and admire the rest?

And at last the peepers, telling those who understand their language: "Spring is here!"

Bethany knows the tradition between us and the Krutches, in the days before they moved to Arizona. She has taken over their part of our pleasant custom, and one day in March, if she hears the little announcers of spring before we do, the telephone will ring and it will be Bethany saying: "Happy peepers!"

It Ain't Necessarily So

THROUGHOUT THIS BOOK I have used the term "armchair gardener" with, perhaps, an unsuitable lack of respect. I am aware of the fact that in every field of endeavor we need people who will study and do research work and write about it, so that we can all have a chance to learn what others have found out.

These people tell us many things which we need to know. My quarrel with them is not that they are human and therefore make mistakes; my quarrel is that too often they hand conjectures and surmises to us amateurs and call these things truths. How is a beginner to know whether an expert is correct, or basing his conclusions on too limited a survey, or merely careless?

The working gardeners who have advised me through the years—Scott, John, Rex, Carl Warren of Joseph Harris and Co., and the local farmers—never led me astray. They told me a fact, or presented a theory, or said they didn't know.

As our experience grows we learn to read the armchair gardeners with a healthy skepticism and, without half trying, catch them in sweeping mis-statements. For instance, here is an article by Charles H. Connors, published in the *New York Herald Tribune*. He has *Rutgers University* printed under his name: that means he is an authority, doesn't it?

He begins by telling us that a gardenia is the last house plant he would choose. In the ordinary household, he says, most buds fall off before they open. Then he tells us to keep the gardenia in the sun all day, giving instructions about setting the pot on something wet, indicating several choices, none of which is simply a pan with water in it. This is an attempt to give the plant a high humidity, which, he informs us, is difficult to attain in an ordinary household. Gardenias are likely to be attacked by mealy worms, he goes on, and you must spray the plants every ten days or two weeks. But when the insects are old, spraying does little good; he tells us how to swab them.

If you read that article would you want a gardenia? If you had one which seemed to be doing all right, wouldn't you begin to feel a little nervous about it?

Harriet Small, to whom I had given a small gardenia plant which I had started from my large one, sent me this clipping. She was full of indignation about it, for her plant was growing rapidly, presenting her with blossoms, never dropping a bud.

If Mr. Connors had begun his article on a more cheerful note, if he had not sounded licked before he started, if he had said that now and then people had bad luck with gardenias but they would have good luck if they would follow his advice, I might have thought: Well, in spite of the fact that mine startles everyone with its size, luxuriance, and almost constant blooming, maybe I'd have even greater success if I'd follow Mr. Connors' advice.

But re-reading his opening paragraph of almost complete defeat, I said to myself: No doubt Mr. Connors of Rutgers University is a very learned man, but there happens to be one little thing he is all mixed up about, and that is gardenias. I thought it was too bad to have an expert discouraging and misleading people, so I wrote him a letter.

I told him I had a fifteen-year-old gardenia doing fine in an ordinary household. It had around seventy-five large, beautiful blossoms each year, it had never dropped a bud, was carefully kept *out* of the sun, and no attention was paid to humidity except to keep it wet and sitting in a pan of water. It had never seen a mealy bug, and had never been sprayed.

I thought it possible that Mr. Connors had friends in our general neighborhood whom he visited and I sent him directions to our place, inviting him to come and have a look at my plant if he happened to be up our way.

He didn't answer my letter, which seemed a pity. I would like to have the feeling that people who write authoritatively on a subject make an effort to learn all they can about that subject.

That is perhaps the basis of my quarrel with experts: in my limited experience with them, they seem to get into a rut and show neither intention nor desire to get out of it.

This is the way I care for my gardenia; nothing could be easier. You need neither spray, nor fertilizer, nor a green thumb. I keep it sitting in a pan which always has water in it, but I also water it from the top. It sits on a low bench in a west window in fall, winter, and early spring where it gets the pale afternoon sun, but there is not much sun when the trees are in leaf. In summer it sits out of doors in almost complete shade. Every leaf that falls off it goes right back in the pot and, when I don't give the flowers away, it gets those, also, after they have turned yellow.

Twice, I think, in the last five years, I have given it a handful of cow manure and once a few spoons of cotton-seed meal. As I understand it, when the leaves of anything turn yellow at a time when they shouldn't, it may indicate a need for nitrogen. Cotton-seed meal supplies that, and so when I thought the leaves looked a little yellow, I gave the plant some meal.

My gardenia has never had any of the "miracle" foods which are supposed to boost plants. It is a very large, fine, healthy plant; each year it gets bigger and more luxuriant. Once in awhile, during the winter, I take a soft tissue and wipe the dust from the leaves. This is not necessary, but the plant is supposed to breathe better if you do, and it certainly looks better.

Ha! some expert says, all this is an accident. That plant just happens to have the perfect environment. Put it in another house and it would begin to behave as Mr. Connors' gardenia does.

That cannot be true. For one thing, Mrs. Maiga, the woman

who gave John the original cuttings, has many beautiful plants.
John learned from her and I learned from him how to care for
them. John had wonderful luck in a house which is quite
different from ours as far as heating and such things are concerned. Joe Krutch had a fine gardenia (mine) which never
dropped a bud. Virginia has it now; it is still letting its buds
reach maturity.

For another thing, my plant has many children and grand-
children, living at my various friends' houses, in ordinary house-
holds but with different environments. John and I are constantly
starting new bushes from slips, and I visit the friends to whom
I give them and have a chance to watch their progress. I don't
know of one failure.

I am so emphatic when I give instructions about what to do,
and particularly what not to do, that, when I gave a plant to
Janet von Dobeneck, she listened carefully and then said:
"You keep it. I'm afraid to take on such a responsibility." She
kept it, of course, and last night she told me it was about to
bloom. Some of the girls to whom I give them bring them over
to sit under the bridal wreath with mine whenever they go
away on vacation; aside from that, they all have different homes.

Someone might raise this question: since all of the gardenias
I have been telling about were started originally from one
plant, might it not be that this is a marvelous strain and these
plants are exceptional?

Here is an answer to that: I know a woman who had a
plant given to her, and for several years kept it in the sun all
day. All of the buds dropped off before they bloomed. When
I first saw it the leaves were all yellow and brown; there was
not a green leaf on it. I asked her to lend it to me and let me
try to revive it.

John took it out of the pot it was in and gave it fresh, rich
dirt from my vegetable garden. This was last June. I put it
under the bridal wreath along with the other gardenias.

It began to leaf out almost miraculously. It was pitifully

lopsided; obviously it had not been turned around often, always the same side reaching toward the light. John cut it back when it began to make leaves, to give it a better shape.

By August it was a fine green plant and had three buds on it which did not drop off, but made lovely blossoms. Its former owner didn't want it back and, while it was in bloom, I gave it to Marjorie and Chester Foley. I saw it in December in their living room. It was then a large, healthy plant.

I believe you can ignore the pessimistic Mr. Connors and have a blooming gardenia if you want one.

Now, shall we have some fun getting annoyed at the experts about tulips? Let us assume that you are a beginner and want a few tulips to brighten your yard each year, to put in a vase, to hand to a poor city person who has none. Let us assume that you do not particularly care to compete with anybody, don't want to show off, cannot spare much money or time for tulips, and would not mind if the third or fourth or tenth season the flowers were somewhat smaller than they were the first year. You want some gay, goodlooking tulips with a minimum of expenditure of time and money.

You buy bulbs and plant them. The next spring you have a fine display. But in the meantime you have read some rather discouraging things. The *Garden Encyclopedia* has informed you: "When the practice of buying new tulip bulbs every year is followed, the bulbs should be dug as soon as they finish flowering, for the longer they stay in the ground, the smaller will be the chances of producing good quality flowers in the same location next year. Those who desire to use the same bulbs again should realize that the second-year bulbs will not be likely to give as good results as would new ones because, even with the best care, the cultural conditions in the average garden do not compare with those used in commercial bulb-growing fields."

You don't feel happy about that, for you had not intended to spend money for new bulbs each year. You decide not to and you read further: "As soon as the foliage is completely withered the bulbs should be lifted." (This is in case you are going to use these same bulbs again.)

You wait for the foliage to wither and find, to your regret, that they do not die until July, looking ugly all that time. In mid-July you dig up the bulbs and now it is too late to put anything else in the bare spot that is left. You could put some perennials there, but that is the place you want to save for tulips.

In the fall you put them back and do this for four seasons, but you are not happy about it. And then you hear (from experts, naturally) that tulips may be planted in the same bed for three years, but, after that, one should choose a new spot for them. You had thought yours had looked the same as always the fourth spring, but they couldn't have, since the authorities had intimated that they wouldn't. You look around for a new bed for them.

Your copy of *The Garden Encyclopedia* is an old edition, and when you see that the September 1954 issue of *Consumer Reports* has an article on bulbs, you read it hopefully. Maybe they will save you some trouble.

No relief in sight. "If the bulbs are taken up every year— *as they should be*—" (italics mine). Not only that: "They should then be reset in soil where no tulips have been grown for several years." And: "—a common cause for their short life is that most people never get around to taking care of them. It is best to lift the bulbs annually—"

You re-read the article; surely the bulbs don't have to be changed to a new bed *every* year. Yes, apparently they should be.

So now it has become a major job and problem: where to put the tulips each year? All because you trusted the experts and didn't strike out brazenly for yourself.

I have a row of tulips about thirty feet long and three feet wide; they are planted three abreast. We put in bulbs twenty-five years ago. I was completely ignorant and followed the rules the first two years. The third year I decided it was too much bother to take up the bulbs and the bed was too ugly for too

long a time. For four years, then, I let them alone and planted
other things in the row with them to take the curse off the
withering tops.

Then, one day, my conscience pricked me and I decided
it was too arrogant to go against the advice of those who knew
so much better than I did. I dug up the whole business and
put the bulbs around in different beds. Everywhere, there were
so many by now, and I gave dozens away.

I let them alone to do as they pleased (my humility didn't
last so very long) and they did splendidly. But I missed my
row of early gayety and, eight years ago, I bought enough
tulip bulbs direct from Holland to fill the original spot. I dug
a trench, carried away all the dirt, and filled the trench with
rich mulch dirt from the vegetable garden, mixed with fresh
manure. *Consumer Reports* says: "—not manure unless it is
very old and well rotted." I planted my tulips hit or miss,
paying no attention to variety or color. *The Garden Encyclopedia*
says no, no, NO, never do that! I planted them six inches deep,
not nine, as *Consumer Reports* says you should do if you are
not going to take them up.

Don't misunderstand my attitude; I was not feeling antag-
onistic, not deliberately going against the rules. Except for the
fresh manure, which I knew all authorities warned you against
in general, I was simply planting some tulip bulbs in the best
way I knew at that time.

That was eight years ago. The bulbs have never been disturbed, the bed has had no fertilizer except mulch, the mulch
is always there although both *Consumer Reports* and *The
Garden Encyclopedia* tell you not to put on mulch until the
ground is well frozen. And I do not rake off "all the old leaves
and dead flower stalks," as Ethel M. Eaton says you must do.

That row of flowers is quite striking and lovely each spring.
This last season I mailed two hundred blossoms at different
times to Mary and Elizabeth (they give them to their friends)
and I gave away another hundred, not counting the ones John
and Art are invited to help themselves to. There are always

some in the house, besides, and at no time did it look as if any had been picked.

I am not entirely clear as to what is supposed to be the disadvantage in growing them my way. Are there fewer flowers? I have hundreds. Are the stems shorter? Mine are long enough for any purpose I can think of. Are the flowers smaller? Mine seem to be normal size. Will the bed die out sooner? Mine has lasted eight years, and if it is out there dying right this minute (which I think unlikely) I have had eight years of lovely gay tulips with no work at all since the original planting. And the bed is always beautiful for, since I don't dig up the bulbs, I can have other flowers growing there too.

I don't say that everyone can do this; I don't say that anyone else can. I don't know. It may be a freak, it may be that I am a genius, it may be what the insurance companies call an act of God, this time a pleasant one, but—well, you know, I doubt all that very much.

Here is a good question: why don't the experts give the layman a choice? Why don't they say: *This* is the way to have show tulips, but there is also a way to have very pretty tulips without trouble, expense, or ugliness of a withering bed? (If there *is* a difference; I am not convinced that there is.)

They do tell you that you *can* have some tulips of a sort for a while if you never take them up, but they disapprove of them. They do not tell you that you can have lots of lovely tulips for years without doing a thing except to plant them once. They must know it. It cannot be possible that they are simply ignorant. Not the *experts!*

When I first thought about this chapter I took it for granted that I would have to spend some time looking for misinformation to quote. I kept putting it off; then one day at a friend's house I glanced at a copy of *Better Homes and Gardens Garden Book.* I found:

On page 330 they tell us that mulches are not for vegetables where the soil temperature rises slowly. I have had won-

derful results with mulch for eleven years in those circumstances.

On page 353 they tell you that corn roots go deep, so the deeper
you spade or plow the better. I never plow or spade at all;
I have splendid corn, usually two fine ears to a stalk.

On page 359 they tell you that mulch should be spread after
the soil is thoroughly stirred. I never stir the soil; I get
excellent results.

On page 362 they tell you to use peppers while they are still
green. Why? Nutritionists tell us they have more vitamins
when they are red. We think they also taste better.

Shortly after I had read and made note of the above, I ran
across a letter in *The Rural New Yorker* from a man saying
that for thirty years he had grown muskmelons, had produced
beautiful ones with a fine aroma, but with no flavor. He had
thrown bushels of them away. He asked the reason.

They answered that it was apparently due to disease infec-
tion and told him what to do. After the experience I had had
with melons I thought that was the wrong answer. I asked
both Rex and Carl Warren of Joseph Harris and Company about
it and they both said that a healthy-looking vine producing fine-
looking melons could not be diseased. They thought there must
be some other reason.

The question I am raising here is: Should an authority on
gardening think it is possible for diseased vines to produce fine-
looking melons?

Sometime later I chanced on an article in the same magazine
by Ethel M. Eaton. There are eleven different things in it which
she tells the reader to do. Six of these I never do, and four out
of the six I think it is unwise to do. Two out of the remaining
five are about flowers I don't grow and have no opinion about.

I don't read farm and garden magazines often. These items
I have given you are not chosen, I am sorry to say, after reading
hundreds or even a dozen articles. They are almost the only
ones I have read since I started to think about this chapter,

and to me it is shocking that with so little research I could find so many questionable statements. This is too bad, because the printed word is so persuasive. For instance, Juanita Peck—intelligent, sensible, practical—had seen my mulched garden many times but didn't abandon the old, cumbersome method until she had read my article about it in *Organic Gardening and Farming*. Then she cried with enthusiasm, "I'm going to mulch!" And did.

I do not at all say that I am right and the others are wrong, but I do say that in all the cases mentioned, their advice is against what I am doing, and I am getting first-class results. Once again I ask the question: Can't the people who write about gardening say this is *a* way, instead of saying this is *the* way? Can't they learn to make use of that little word "perhaps"?

These dogmatic rules which may turn out to be wrong or only half right make it tough going for the beginner. And yet a beginner must have guidance. I suppose he learns fairly early not to lean on the armchair gardeners too heavily.

Gardening is like cooking: read the recipe and then use your head. A dash of skepticism can do no harm. Go lightly on caution, heavily on adventure, and see what comes out. If you make a mistake, what of it? That is one way to learn, and tomorrow is another day.

We Shall Come Rejoicing

HARVEST.

There is the harvest moon, and there are fall festivals in celebration of the gathering of crops, but actually we are "bringing in the sheaves" from the first dandelion we snare in April to the last kale or collards or brussels sprouts we brush the snow from before we take it into the kitchen. If you can or freeze your products or have a root cellar you will find that gardening is a constant, satisfying routine of reaping the rewards of your labor.

Whichever you choose today—fresh garden peas, a large white head of cauliflower, fine crisp corn, some brilliant peppers, canned tomatoes, or frozen asparagus—you can be proud to serve it, asking it: What lesser thing would I be preparing for dinner tonight if you and I had not collaborated?

Is gardening worth while? If you ask that question the answer is: Possibly not, for you. Because if you are a gardener in your heart that is something you will never doubt.

Before we came to live in the country I had been donating a large part of each day to helping those people who were trying to make a better, happier world. For lack of opportunity that stopped, more or less, when we came here, and sometimes I would wonder if I had failed in my duty to humanity.

I said something to Rex about it and he answered: "Can you do anything more fundamental than to raise food? Even Einstein has to eat."

I liked that answer, but I was still disturbed enough to mention it to Scott. He said: "You are proving that a person can live a happy, sane, and simple life in a mixed-up world. Isn't that constructive enough?"

I hoped it was for I was happy. I had never done any work I disliked (and I had done quite a lot of different kinds of things), but nothing had ever before so completely combined exhilaration, peace, and a conviction that I was producing something valuable and necessary. I believe that to a large degree this feeling of satisfaction is a common one among farmers.

In any phase of life it is the disasters which make the head-lines. To outsiders, a farmer's life is apt to seem either dull and monotonous or full of frustrations and calamities.

As far as the dullness goes, they could not be more mistaken. Besides the obvious thrills in the country, which the city dweller sees and understands, there are others which no outsider could fully appreciate.

The frost is out of the ground. . . . I've put my peas in, do you think it's too early? . . . I got the hay in just before that downpour. . . . I'm sure the ground is dry enough to plant. . . . The corn is ready to cut—four days earlier than I expected. . . . I had a pumpkin so big I couldn't lift it. . . . I was amazed this morning when I saw there was asparagus ready to pick. . . . Do you know anyone who could use some fine cauliflower plants? . . .

I should think it would be difficult, if not impossible, for a city dweller to have any conception of the pleasant excitement running through these remarks. To the ones who are saying them and hearing them they are brimming over with the exhilaration of life, growth, of forging ahead.

Farmers love and appreciate beauty. I doubt if many of them could tell a Rembrandt from a Corot. Some of them couldn't tell you if Rembrandt and Corot were painters, composers, wrestlers, or prize Herefords. But they know a scarlet tanager from a cardinal, a goldfinch from a wild canary.

They are seldom too busy to stop a moment and gaze across

the field at a wild plum just beginning to flower among the tender yellow green of early leaves and darker evergreens. They appreciate the beauty of a deer, a raccoon, a freshly plowed field; they find time to plant and care for flowers. They love the smell of the turned-over earth, of the morning air, of freshly cut hay. They wear dirty overalls sometimes, but the filth of the city offends them.

They love the sound of crickets, katydids, the songs of birds, the sharp and gentle noises of the night. They like the feel of the earth; they like to pass their hands slowly over a satiny piece of wood or smooth gourd. Their taste for fine flavors is highly developed. They may not know which wine "goes" with which meat, but they would not eat an ear of city corn unless they were exceedingly hungry and there was nothing else to eat. They wouldn't eat fresh strawberries in February. With all their five senses they are discriminating and appreciative.

This is really true; I am not making it up. I have no reason to make it up; I tell it because I believe the average city dweller thinks of the farmer as an overworked, rather pathetic, uncultured person.

He is sometimes overworked. He is, in my observation, no more pathetic than any other class. By my definition of culture (which I just this minute made up) he is cultured. My definition is: getting a great deal of discriminating enjoyment out of the five senses.

Working in the garden gives me something beyond enjoyment of the senses. I am not prepared to say whether it gives this same thing to farmers and other gardeners, but I am inclined to believe that it does. It gives me a profound feeling of inner peace. Nothing here is in a hurry. There is no rush toward accomplishment, no blowing of trumpets. Here is the great mystery of life and growth. Everything is changing, growing, aiming at something, but silently, unboastfully, taking its time.

There is no competition, no criticism in a garden, and yet where, in so small and crowded a space, could you find so many different things, looking, seeming, behaving so differently?

The carrots and parsnips modestly hide the most important part of themselves under the ground. The cabbage becomes a big green ball, the tomato plants make smaller balls which turn red. The corn, it would seem, might frighten the gentle parsley by shooting away up in the air. But the parsley is not afraid.

The corn is not arrogant about its superior height: it doesn't shout: "Do as I do, you little runts. *Be* somebody!" Peppers do not ridicule the carrots for hiding in the ground, calling them cowards. The parsnips don't accuse the gay red-and-green peppers and tomatoes of showing off.

The asparagus doesn't form an organization to fight un-asparagus vegetables. It has been in the garden many, many years longer than any of the other things, but it doesn't tell a single one of them to go back where it came from. Live and let live is the motto. Each one does the best it can, unobtrusively, uncritically, and so there is peace in the garden. Peace and results.

If you are alone and work quietly you will find that you feel a part of these living, growing things. You lift a bit of mulch and there are the repulsive little earthworms, diligently doing their great work of keeping the soil in good condition, so that everything will grow. If you compare yourself to them, you need not feel ashamed, but you may feel humble.

You touch the warm, moist earth and it feels so good—so good. You want to be—you hope you are—one half as useful as an earthworm.

As a child I had high ambitions. A great writer and a great actress—I was going to be those two things at least. Also a great pianist, if I could get hold of a piano to practice on, a great singer if I could learn to carry a tune.

Now when I am in the garden my ambition is a little higher. I want to live as quietly, modestly, uncritically and usefully as a beet, a carrot, a tomato. I want to do my small part and not interfere with those who are doing their part. I want to live in uncritical peace with my fellow man.

Now there is a slight stir in the garden; a light breeze is

passing by. It carries a message to all living, growing things. The corn hears and understands and rustles its leaves in gentle excitement as it murmurs softly but clearly so that all may hear: "We shall come rejoicing."